The Cruciform Church

*Becoming a Cross-Shaped People
in a Secular World*

Second Edition

by
C. Leonard Allen

Acknowledgment is made for permission to quote from the following works: Wendell Berry, *Collected Poems* (San Francisco, Calif: North Point, 1985), pp. 159,209; Excerpt from "Choruses From The Rock" in *Collected Poems, 1909-1962* by T.S. Eliot, copyright 1936 by Harcourt Brace Jovanovich, Inc., copyright © 1964, 1963 by T.S. Eliot, reprinted by permission of the publisher, p.101; Graham Green, *The Power and the Glory* (New York: Bantam Books, 1972), p. 123; and Cynthia Ozick, *Metaphor and Memory* (New York: Alfred A. Knopf, 1989), pp. 265-69,283.

All Scripture citations are from the Revised Standard Version unless otherwise indicated.

Typesetting and Cover Design, Mel Ristau/Design
Illustration, Mel Ristau
Printed in the United States of America

ISBN 0-89112-098-X,Paper
ISBN 0-89112-099-8,Cloth
Library of Congress Card Number 89-82537

Second Edition   1 2 3 4 5

*In a word, as God's dear children, try to be like him,
and live in love as Christ loved you, and gave himself up
on your behalf.*

Ephesians 5:1-2

What is left of the Gospel, if you take away the cross?

Charles L. Loos (1869)

The wisdom of the cross lies hidden in a deep mystery.

Martin Luther (1530)

To Thomas H. Olbricht

Christian scholar and promoter of scholarship

Contents

Preface

Cru'ci-form—shaped or arranged in a cross.
—Webster's Collegiate Dictionary

There are three things I would like to say to readers as they begin this book.

First, this book continues the project that began with two previous books, *Discovering Our Roots: The Ancestry of Churches of Christ* (with Richard T. Hughes) and *The Worldly Church: A Call for Biblical Renewal* (with Hughes and Michael Weed). The first book attempted to show how the past has shaped Churches of Christ. The second book looked at the challenges of the present. This third book, while engaging both past and present, primarily points to the future.

Second, the title of the book calls for a bit of explanation. In choosing the word *cruciform*, I overrode the objections of several friends who thought the word too strange and new. Most of them liked the word but feared that it simply would not communicate with some people. Perhaps not. And perhaps the title of a book is not the place to introduce a new word.

I chose the word, however, because I believe it wonderfully and concisely conveys the vision of what Christ's church can and must be. I chose the word in hope that this image might become the dominant image by which Churches of Christ speak of identifying the New Testament church.

Toward this end, I have structured this book around five theological "identity points":

1) the way we read and interpret the Bible (chapters 2 and 3)
2) the way we understand the God revealed in Scripture (chapter 4)
3) the place we give to Christ and his cross (chapter 5)
4) the stance of the church toward "the world" (chapter 6)
5) the extent to which we portray Christlike character (chapter 7)

The cord tying all these chapters together is the biblical imperative to lift up Christ crucified and to let the church be known primarily by its faithfulness in following the way of the cross.

Third, I want to acknowledge my debt to Churches of Christ. One of the most basic convictions underlying this book is the necessity of locating oneself in time, of recognizing and working with what one has received from the past. So I must say that my faith—and indeed, much of my life—has been shaped deeply by this heritage. I have not yet discovered just how deeply. I doubt that I ever will.

It dawned on me some time ago that even as I question and critique some aspects of my heritage, I remain very much a child of it. However much I might want to stand free from the influence of tradition and thus be free to start from scratch, I cannot do so, for the long reaches of the past are too much with me.

My heritage among Churches of Christ I view neither as a straitjacket that rigidly confines me nor as a light outer garment of no consequence that I can strip off at will. Rather, I view it as a worn but still sturdy garment of faith that (with careful alterations) can yet serve me well.

It is one of the great conceits of our time to imagine that we can sweep away the past and simply begin all over again at the beginning. We cannot. For in a thousand and one ways (many of them unknown to us) our past and its traditions have made us what we are and given us our identity. This book therefore rests upon the conviction that we will find freedom to change, grow, and respond to new challenges only as we care about the past and listen to its voices.

My debts in the writing of this book are many. I owe a special debt to three dear friends: Richard Hughes, professor of religion at Pepperdine University; Jack Reese, professor in the College of Biblical Studies at Abilene Christian University; and Harold Shank, preaching minister of the Highland Street Church of Christ in Memphis, Tennessee.

Richard encouraged me to begin the project and helped me conceptualize it. Jack encouraged, listened (sometimes late into the night), and offered wise advice all along the way. And Harold spent many hours responding to my work in very helpful ways. All three read and critiqued the complete manuscript. Without their friendship, encouragement, and expertise I could not have written this book.

In addition I must mention several others who read all or parts of the manuscript and graciously offered me their special expertise: Bill Love who ministers with the Bering Drive Church of Christ in Houston, Texas; Tom Geer and Gailyn Van Rheenen of the ACU Bible faculty; and Darryl Tippens of the ACU English Department. The chapter endnotes in this book amply testify to many other debts that I owe.

I also thank Roberta Brown, secretary in the College of Biblical Studies, for her support of my work and the expert assistance that went well beyond the call of duty. My graduate assistants Sean Niestrath and Andy Wall also provided invaluable help checking sources, proofreading, and preparing the manuscript.

Finally, I thank my wife Holly for caring about my work enough to put up with the demands it placed on her and on our family. I must thank her also for making light of it at those times when I let it become too heavy.

C. Leonard Allen
December 1989

1

The Search for Identity

> *...What we owe the future*
> *is not a new start, for we can only begin*
> *with what has happened. We owe the future*
> *the past, the long knowledge*
> *that is the potency of time to come.*
> *That makes of a man's grave a rich furrow.*
>
> —*Wendell Berry (1975)*

> *The golden age only comes to men when they*
> *have, if only for a moment, forgotten gold.*
>
> —*G. K. Chesterton (1932)*

In his book *Watership Down*, author Richard Adams created an intriguing world inhabited by rabbits. The story focuses on the adventures of a scraggly band of rabbits who leave a large established warren in order to find themselves a new home.[1]

Among them is Hazel, who later becomes the leader, and Fiver, Hazel's strange brother who possesses the gifts of a seer. They are joined by several others: Bigwig, an ambitious rabbit who seeks power and position, Pipkin, who is small and weak and constantly needing help, and Blackberry, who possesses great intelligence and wisdom. Together they leave their warren because of Fiver's cryptic warning that it will be destroyed. And together they establish a new warren at Watership Down.

The reader quickly learns that rabbits live in a dangerous world—a world of trappers, hunters, predatory animals, and threatening rabbits. To survive in such a world they must band together, pooling all their wit and cunning and learning to appreciate one another's gifts.

Furthermore, their survival depends upon learning and retelling the stories of the rabbits who have gone before them. For in those stories they learn about the dangers rabbits face and gain the skills to negotiate those dangers. From those stories they learn to face a dangerous environment in a manner appropriate to rabbits.

The motley group of rabbits that form Watership Down cherish the stories of El-ahrairah, a great hero among the early rabbits. The stories tell of his cleverness and wit. They recount with delight and humor the tricks he used to outwit his enemies and gain advantage for his fellow rabbits.

The telling of those stories binds them together. It helps them work together and value the gifts of even the weakest members of the group. Bigwig learns to trust the others. Blackberry learns that his impeccable logic is not always sufficient. They all learn to care for Pipkin in his weakness. The stories form their identity as a community.

But the time came when the rabbits encountered a warren that no longer maintained the traditions of El-ahrairah. These rabbits had forgotten how to tell the stories and thus how to work together and to appreciate each rabbit's gifts. As a result they had grown weak and disoriented. They recognized no leader—each one simply did as he pleased. They lacked the skills to recognize danger and to defend themselves. So they easily fell prey to the farmers' traps. By failing to treasure and retell the stories of El-ahrairah, they had forgotten the ways of wild rabbits.

In his story Adams tells us something not so much about rabbits as about people. He shows the importance of forging links with those who have gone before. He underscores the vital place of traditions in living well and in maintaining a strong sense of identity.

Losing the Past

One of the chief characteristics of modern secular culture is the loss of this sense of connectedness to the past. The spirit of individualism, rampant in our time, says: "You can be whatever you choose to be. Forget the past. Disregard its traditions. Dismiss its stories. Accept none of its constraints. Bear no responsibilities for its failures. For you are perfectly free to order your own life, to go your own way." As Lewis Smedes put it, "our culture urges us not to define our life in terms of past commitments but in terms of present needs and future possibilities."[2]

As this happens the sense of personal or group identity erodes, for as Alasdair MacIntyre insists, one's identity is always rooted in a particular story or tradition. "I am someone's son or daughter, someone else's cousin or uncle. . . . I inherit from the past of my family, my city, my nation, a variety of debts, inheritances, rightful expectations and obligations. . . . I am born with a past; and to try to cut myself off from that past, in the individualist mode, is to deform my present relationships."[3]

A strong sense of identity requires a sense of continuity with the past. Particularly in times of rapid change (like ours), it requires what Robert Bellah has called a "community of memory." Without such communities we grow increasingly disoriented. We lose the ability to recognize dangers and respond to them in ways appropriate to human beings. We lose the capacity to sustain our ideals and commitments; we become more utilitarian, more prone to let the current status quo shape our identity.

The effects of losing the past appear strikingly in the mainline Protestant churches of the 1960s. Captivated by a consumerist economy, many churches rushed to find ever more relevant ways of appealing to the culture. In the process, they devalued or even scorned their historic traditions. "Modernist protestantism," Leonard Sweet argues, "remained hopelessly estranged from the voices of its past, its members having almost entirely forgotten how to live historically in conversation with their classic traditions."[4]

Today we among Churches of Christ find ourselves facing a similar situation. We too face a kind of identity crisis. Although many factors contribute to it, three seem particularly significant.

First, there is the simple fact that all religious traditions change from one generation to the next. Changes may be subtle, but the very process of passing on a set of beliefs inevitably alters them. Thus, we find that Churches of Christ today are not the same as they were in the 1940s and 1950s and that those of the 1940s and 1950s were significantly different from those of the 1870s.

Second, this inevitable change has been accelerated in this generation by the virtually complete breakup of the rural world (or ethos) which originally shaped the identity of Churches of Christ in the late nineteenth century. One recent scholar, in a study of the sweeping agricultural and economic changes that thoroughly reshaped the South between 1920 and 1960, spoke of "rural worlds lost."[5] In the demise of those worlds, we lost part of our past.

Third, the secular ethos of our time, with its rampant individualism and pluralism, now places enormous pressures upon us. Drawn into the religious marketplace and pressured by the consumer's addiction to newness, we are further cut off from our historic roots.

Accepting a Past

How should we respond to our identity crisis? Like the rabbits of Watership Down we must forge links with our past. We must learn to tell its stories. The thesis of this book is that by facing our past and learning to appropriate it, we can chart with renewed clarity our course for the future. Doing this means taking the step of locating ourselves within time. It means acknowledging that we indeed have a past, a human tradition, and that to a significant degree we are products of that past.

But what may appear at first as a simple task really is not. For our heritage, the Stone-Campbell movement, arose out of a profound disenchantment with the past. Like many Americans in the early decades of American nationhood, Barton Stone, Alexander Campbell, Walter Scott, and other early forebears sought to dismiss the past with all its limitations. The past had bequeathed only spiritual confusion, moral decay, sectarian wrangling, and a deadening traditionalism. So they sought to sweep away the confusion and decay, to abandon the polluted stream for the pure spring.

This attitude toward the past characterized the early movement. Sometimes it found striking expression. Campbell could write, for example, that "On the subject of religion I am fully persuaded that nothing but the inspired scriptures ought ever to have been published."[6] Nineteen centuries of Christian reflection and writing, in other words, served only to obscure and inhibit the practice of true Christianity.

Propelled by such an attitude toward the past, restoration movements like ours easily develop a kind of historylessness.[7] By this term I refer to the perception that, while other churches or movements are snared in the web of profane history, one's own church or movement stands above mere human history. One's own movement partakes only of the perfections of the first age, the sacred time of pure beginnings. While other movements lurch along through the quagmire of time, one's own movement strolls easily on the firm streets of eternity. While others stagger under the load of traditions bequeathed them by the past, one's own group has no real history and thus no load of tradition to shoulder.

This sense of historylessness works in powerful and subtle ways. In the process it creates exhilarating (and damaging) illusions. Among Churches of Christ it often has meant that we simply discounted eighteen centuries of Christianity as, at worst, a diseased tumor or, at best, an instructive failure.

And not surprisingly, the same attitude has led many people among Churches of Christ to dismiss their own history as itself irrelevant. For after all, if our origins come entirely from the Bible and our churches are New Testament churches, nothing more and nothing less, then we really need not bother ourselves with the recent past. Indeed, it too might simply serve to distract us from our true calling.

But clearly some people among Churches of Christ have bothered with the past. Some have searched through the annals of their own restoration movement and on occasion ranged further afield to the larger story of Christianity through the ages. But even here, most often, one can discern a kind of historylessness at work. To be sure, it is much more subtle than simply dismissing the past. Here one attends to the past, sometimes even with great energy and diligence, but in the process one lays upon the past a preformed pattern or schema— a traditional pattern of the church's fall and restoration.

This pattern then becomes the key that quickly and simply makes sense of the past. It functions like a procrustean bed: one stretches and trims history's main actors and movements to fit the pattern. For one does not seek so much to find a complex and tangled story told in black, white, and many shades of gray, but a simple story of the good and the bad, the right and the wrong, the true and the untrue. One wants to separate the scattering of good guys from the host of bad guys, making it unmistakeably clear just who stands with us and who against us.

The restorationist can do this due to one important factor: he easily assumes that he himself is not really part of the history he surveys, that he is not fully part of the historical process with all its limitations and strictures. He actually stands above history, disentangled from its sticky web. He dwells on a lofty overlook, there standing as it were among Plato's timeless Forms and with them measuring the change and decay that constantly settles over all things temporal.

Such is the allure of the sense of historylessness: either to dismiss church history altogether or, more subtly, to pass judgment upon it as if we ourselves were not part of its stream. In either case, most all of Christian history finally becomes little more than a tragic story of decay and corruption, a dark plot in which one can indeed discern people who seem to possess noble motives and admirable courage but all of whom are finally exposed either as villains or as naive pawns, and all implicated in the high crime of poisoning the pure stream of truth.

This sense of historylessness has predominated in our movement. And that predominance has inhibited and distorted our theological efforts in several ways.

For one thing, such attitudes toward the past have given rise to unfair and inaccurate views of the past. They have caused us to approach history as polemics and as hagiography. The two approaches usually go hand in hand. The polemical approach caricatures those outside our movement to prove them wrong;

the hagiographical approach idealizes and idolizes those within the movement to prove us right. In this way we typically made short work of pre-restoration history. Most often we plundered it for case studies of corruption, for examples of "human invention," and for glimpses of aborted restorations.

In the process we sought not so much to understand earlier Christian movements in all their complexity. We sought rather to decry them or on occasion simply to ridicule them. For they obviously ran in the stream of profane history, swept along by little more than human willfulness and ignorance.

But our movement was different. It did not run in any wide and turgid stream. Rather, it gushed directly out of the spring, forming only a crystal clear pool around it. Our leaders were larger-than-life figures, religious geniuses, people who never mixed eternal truth with temporal clay. And so we often constructed romantic chronicles, pitting unmixed Truth against the hosts of ignorance and Untruth. It was an exciting story, almost the stuff of epics and legends.

Sometimes this approach to the past was subtle and somewhat sophisticated, sometimes it was bald and unwincing. Consider, for example, John F. Rowe's widely read work of 1884 entitled *A History of Reformatory Movements Resulting in a Restoration of the Apostolic Church* (by 1913 it had gone through nine editions). Though unoriginal in its basic interpretation, Rowe's work served to popularize the simple restoration schema of history and make it a staple of restoration preaching and polemics.

Rowe charged that the sixteenth-century reformers "never made any attempt to return to apostolic practice, nor did these Reformers even suggest the idea of reproducing the Church of Christ as established by the apostles." But Alexander Campbell, in contrast, "sought the complete *restoration* of apostolic principles and practices, and did actually raise up a body of people identical with the primitive Christians, both in faith and practice." Campbell, "having broken away from all traditional trammels," brought about "an entire restoration of the apostolic order of things."[8]

The problem with Rowe's work is not that he criticized the Protestant reformers or even that he rejected aspects of their theology. Rather, the problem is that he failed to understand what they said and why they said it. Rowe in fact shows almost no understanding whatsoever of the central theological issues at stake in the reformation movements of the sixteenth century. Add to that, furthermore, the audacity of claiming that Campbell created a group "identical with the primitive Christians." Thus, what at first one might take as an impressively factual narrative actually turns out to be an exercise in polemics and hagiography.

This approach to the Christian past held sway from pulpit and platform, for it proved an effective tool in arguing that, while other movements were mainly products of human history, ours was not. N. B. Hardeman, prominent preacher and educator of the early twentieth century, provides a ready example. Hardeman employed Rowe's schema extensively in his five series of "Tabernacle Sermons" preached between 1923 and 1942. As with Rowe, the result was serious distortion of the past.

Take Hardeman's presentation of Martin Luther, for instance. He praised Luther for his courage and conviction but in the process misconstrued Luther's theological concerns almost beyond recognition. Luther's sole contribution, Hardeman noted flatly, was that he "gave to the world an open Bible." Hardeman then added: "When you want to study Lutheranism you have no more use for the Bible than you have for an almanac."

John Calvin likewise gets distorted. Hardeman, like many others who used the past polemically, did not distinguish Calvin's thought from what later was called Calvinism. This later Calvinism, especially in its American frontier version, often was a pedantic and doctrinaire thing with a somewhat tenuous connection to John Calvin's own theology. More importantly, Hardeman, like Rowe before him, shows little awareness of how Reformed theology evolved or why, and no awareness whatsoever of the intense concern for restoration of biblical forms and practices that characterized the Reformed tradition throughout much of its history.[9]

Rowe and Hardeman provide fairly typical examples of how Churches of Christ have dealt with the Christian past.

When not simply dismissing it, we have typically used the past polemically by laying a preformed pattern upon it. In this way we short-circuited the arduous work and the considerable measure of sympathy one needs to let the past speak clearly in the present.

Such an assessment, I realize, may appear somewhat irreverent. If it does, then we must confront a most important question: what place should critical engagement with our past (or tradition) occupy in our efforts to live responsibly and faithfully under God? Or to put it differently, can we bear to approach our own history as part of the stream of real human history, marked like all real human history by temporality, contingency, and finitude?

A most fundamental theological question lies at the heart of these other questions: Can we face up to our time-bound, creaturely, and sinful status before the Creator and Lord of all history? Can we accept the fact that we, like every other human being, have a past and partake of its limitations? Or must we harbor the heady illusion of historylessness, the illusion that we have burst the bonds of finitude to soar above this mortal sphere?

Engaging the Past

Only as we accept a past can we begin to engage it. Only as we grow conscious of the human tradition that has nurtured our faith and shaped the way we read the Bible can we assess that tradition, critique it, renew it, and when necessary move beyond it. Seen in this light, critical engagement with our past becomes a fundamental part of our faithfulness to it. It also becomes a fundamental task in maintaining our identity as a restoration movement.

When I speak of *critical engagement* with the past, I must first be clear about what I mean by *critical*. By critical I do not mean carping or cutting down. I do not mean belittling or demeaning. I do not mean a spirit of fault-finding. Not at all. Rather, I mean the "effort to see a thing clearly and truly in order to judge it fairly" (Webster). I refer particularly to the disciplined task of placing historical figures and movements in the context of their times and then respecting the complex and often ironic relationship between them.

When we engage the past critically we do not seek quick and easy condemnation of the past (as with polemics), nor do we seek quick and easy vindication of it (as with hagiography). We do not seek to marshall supporting evidence for our own theological position. We are *critical* in that we seek, as best we can, to understand the past on its own terms, not ours. We approach it with sympathy and imagination, and do not shrink from questioning cherished interpretations.

We must learn to be critical in this sense, for without it we easily play rude tricks upon the dead. We deftly twist and bend the past to serve our present concerns, to support our own vested interests. We easily impose our own agenda upon it.

So when we engage the past critically we seek first and foremost to understand the past, all the while knowing that we too cannot escape fully our own limited perspectives (since we ourselves are part of history's stream). Even though we see in the past all sorts of intellectual shortcomings and moral failures, we attempt to treat the people of the past with all the respect we can muster, for we sense that we too are made of much the same stuff.

The problem is that we are not accustomed to approaching the past—especially our own past—in this way. We may well find it unsettling, disturbing. To some it may look like "bashing the pioneers."

But remember our spiritual forebears. What if Barton Stone, Thomas Campbell, Alexander Campbell, and Walter Scott had been unwilling to critique the tradition that brought them to faith in Christ, that nurtured and sustained them for many years? What if they had shrunk from the task of questioning that tradition for the sake of truth as they understood it?

The fact is that our tradition was born in sharp, even radical dissent from established or traditional norms. But in the succeeding century and a half we often have found ourselves in the ironic situation of being a movement founded on a radical questioning of tradition unwilling to question its own tradition (or allow others to). One point at least seems clear: there is a sense in which we will be true to the tradition that nourished us in the faith only as we ourselves respectfully critique it.

But not only will we be true to the tradition when we critically engage it. More importantly, we will be more faithful in our efforts to interpret Scripture and bring its truth to bear upon our struggles with a secular culture. Let me now be more specific about why.

(1) *Critical engagement with the past makes us self-conscious about our dependence upon traditions from the past.* The first challenge here, as we have seen, is simply recognizing that we do indeed stand in a human tradition, for our historylessness has blinded us to that fact. Our forebears often denied any complicity in human traditions, claiming to be only a people of the Book. They wanted nothing to do with mere traditions. They wanted only the Truth. It was a yearning that, for most of us, lies near the heart of the spiritual quest.

But the sweeping claim to have escaped the taint of all human tradition does not result in a traditionless or culture-free faith. It results only in a faith even more vulnerable to unconscious traditionalism. F. J. A. Hort put it well: "The air is thick with bastard traditions which carry us captive unawares while we seem to ourselves to be exercising our freedom and instinct for truth."[10] Hort here points to one of the chief pitfalls of restoration movements: the tendency to develop powerful traditions propelled by the illusion of existing without tradition.

So first we must simply recognize that we are part of a human tradition. And that is a big step. But once we take that step, we immediately face another crucial step: we must critique our tradition. We must do so simply because it is in part a human tradition, and human traditions—or so many of our forebears believed—are always tainted. If we are unable to criticize our traditions, we will simply remain captive to them. We will harbor illusions or pretensions, and thus tend to absolutize (or make idols of) our own limited tradition.

(2) *Critical engagement with the past also forces us to deal with other traditions in a new way.* As we have seen, a critical attitude toward the past means that we take Christian traditions other than our own with great seriousness. We do not treat them condescendingly or sneer at them or say to ourselves, "How

could people be so blind! How could they be so stubborn or stupid!" Rather, we grant them what we ourselves wish to be granted: sincerity and zeal, honesty and intelligence. With sympathy and imagination, we witness their struggles to take Scripture seriously and to follow God faithfully. We attempt to hear their questions, not simply to make them answer ours.

Certainly that is an arduous and unsettling task. But when we make the effort, something important happens. Through this process we gain new clarity on our own heritage. When we view tradition A (our own) alongside traditions B, C, and D, we will begin to see dimensions of tradition A that we probably never saw before. These other traditions raise new questions, and that helps us as we constructively critique our own tradition in light of Scripture.[11]

The effect of such engagement might best be described as a theological loss of innocence. By that I mean a dawning awareness of one's own rootedness in history with all the limitations that entails. Responsible theological work depends to a considerable degree upon just such a loss of innocence. For if we naively assume that we are fresh and pure, that we stand above worldly compromise and spiritual failure, that we espouse only the Truth and nothing but the Truth, then we lose the capacity for self-criticism, for repentance, and thus for spiritual growth.

(3) *Critical engagement with the past thus reminds us, when we forget, that biblical interpretation (or theology) is always a human enterprise.* Accepting our status as finite, time-bound mortals, we must also accept the finite and therefore revisable status of our theological pronouncements. Theology, in fact, might be defined as human interpretation of divine revelation. God has revealed himself in history and in Scripture, but our interpretation of that revelation takes place within time, under the conditions of creaturely finitude.

For all his protests against theology and theologians, Alexander Campbell himself wrote theology—a great deal of it in fact. He even wrote a book entitled *The Christian System* (1835), where he tried to lay out in a somewhat systematic way his interpretation of the Christian faith. But it was partly (maybe even mostly) the Christian system and partly the Campbell system. (How much of one or the other depends to a considerable degree upon how one views the tradition which Mr. Campbell did so much to inaugurate.)[12]

Such an awareness teaches us that, while we acknowledge God's great claims upon us, we make modest claims for our theology. It teaches us that we must continue our efforts with humility, prayer, and the encouragement of others who also attempt to live out the Christian commitment. We can continue our quest with vigor and excitement, welcoming new and deeper insights and revising older, settled ones in the process, because we know that it is not finally our theology that saves us but the gracious work of God proclaimed in the gospel.

Appropriating the Past

Thus far I have focused on the importance of facing the fact that we indeed stand within a human tradition. Responsible theological work, I suggested, depends upon such an awareness. But this very awareness brings with it a certain danger. One may become so keenly aware of the humanness of the tradition that one is tempted to reject it.

One may perceive serious theological distortions, for example, or discern narrowness and intolerance. One may find overwhelming ironies in the movement (for example, the grandiose plan for unity, yet the runaway fragmentation that ensued). One may be frustrated by institutional intransigence. One may thereby grow disillusioned, longing to brush aside such a past, to banish the tradition, to find newness and simplicity. One may nourish the dream of starting all over again.

I well understand such a longing, for I have felt it strongly at times. But I believe we make a grave mistake in thinking that we can simply put our past behind us, unburden ourselves of its weight, and start over again. For we are not gods, you and I. We do not possess the power to begin our worlds over again; rather, we are creatures situated within one time and one place, bound to work with what has been given us. We find ourselves part of lives and events that have chosen us. We have not chosen them.

Those of us whose faith has been formed among Churches of Christ cannot simply dismiss our past. That past has happened and to a considerable degree has made us what we are. Furthermore, those who do attempt to blot out or lop off their past may well prove themselves, by that very act, a child of the tradition. For after all, that is how restoration traditions tend to deal with tradition—they lop it off, wave the magic wand, act as if what has happened makes little difference.

The trouble is that we never quite rid ourselves of the past. We can try, but we will still carry our past with us in ways we do not fully perceive. One may spend one's life renouncing a heritage but—mark it down—even that renunciation will be shaped by the very heritage it seeks to renounce. Accepting what has been given us from the past is a mark of our finitude, of our creaturely limits.

Acceptance of a past, however, should not mean undue reverence for that past or an easy compliance with its orthodoxies and strictures. For as the early pioneers of our movement saw so clearly, traditions easily absolutize—and thus make idols of—their own limited perspectives and pronouncements. Therefore, accepting one's tradition (or heritage) means in part caring enough about the tradition to engage it critically, thereby helping preserve and correct the ideals that have sustained it over the generations.

This book rests upon the conviction that maintaining a strong sense of identity among Churches of Christ today will mean seeking a sense of continuity with our past—not rejecting or denying that past, not uncritically embracing it, but responsibly appropriating it.

Toward that end I focus, in the chapters that follow, on five theological "identity points"—five factors that most powerfully shape our identity as a Christian people:

(1) *The way we read Scripture.* Chapter two examines and critiques our traditional way of reading Scripture, then chapter three offers some correctives and new directions.

(2) *The way we view God.* Chapter four examines the secular displacement and domestication of God. It explores the dynamics of idolatry in our lives, then points to the uniqueness of the God Scripture reveals.

(3) *The place we give to the cross of Christ.* Chapter five asks, "How have we among Churches of Christ traditionally

preached the 'word of the cross'? and, How should the cross shape our life together in Christ?"

(4) *Our stance toward the "world."* Chapter six explores the relationship of the church to the world. Looking to our own past, it focuses on the perpetual tension between two biblical imperatives: the call to detach ourselves from worldly values and the call to serve the world in sacrificial ways.

(5) *Our portrayal of Christ-like character.* Chapter seven emphasizes the quality and character of our lives as a fundamental mark of Christian identity, focusing particularly on the virtue of compassion.

Throughout this book I ask, "What have we been?" and "What does God through Scripture call us to become?" Both questions are essential. In the interplay between them we will find new direction and identity.

In one of his verse plays, T. S. Eliot spoke of this process of appropriating the past:

The Church must be forever building, and always
    decaying, and always being restored . . . .
But here upon earth you have the reward of the good and
    ill that was done by those who have gone before you.
And all that was ill you may repair if you walk together in
    humble repentance . . . ;
And all that was good you must fight to keep with hearts
    as devoted as those of your fathers who fought to gain it.
The Church must be forever building, for it is forever
    decaying from within and attacked from without.[13]

Notes

Epigraphs: Wendell Berry, "At a Country Funeral," in *Collected Poems* (San Francisco, Calif.: North Point, 1985), p. 159; G. K. Chesterton, *Sidelights on New London and Newer New York* (New York: Dodd, Mead, 1932), p. 143.

[1]Richard Adams, *Watership Down* (New York: Macmillan, 1972). See also Stanley Hauerwas, "A Story-Formed Community: Reflections on *Watership Down*," in *A Community of Character: Toward a Constructive Christian Social Ethic* (Notre Dame, Ind.: University of Notre Dame, 1981), pp. 9-35.

[2]Lewis Smedes, *Mere Morality: What God Expects from Ordinary People* (Grand Rapids, Mich.: Eerdmans, 1983), p. 161.

[3]Alasdair MacIntyre, *After Virtue*, 2nd ed. (Notre Dame, Ind.: University of Notre Dame, 1984), pp. 220, 221.

[4]Leonard I. Sweet, "The Modernization of Protestant Religion in America," in *Altered Landscapes: Christianity in America, 1935-1985*, ed. David W. Lotz (Grand Rapids, Mich.: Eerdmans, 1989), p. 25. See also Wade Clark Roof and William McKinney, *American Mainline Religion: Its Changing Shape and Future* (New Brunswick, N.J.: Rutgers University, 1987), pp. 72-105.

[5]Jack T. Kirby, *Rural Worlds Lost: The American South, 1920-1960* (Baton Rouge, La.: Louisiana State University, 1988).

[6]Alexander Campbell, "Prefatory Remarks," *Christian Baptist* 4 (August 7, 1826):3.

[7]Sidney Mead proposed a profound sense of "historylessness" as one of the defining themes of American Christianity in the early nineteenth century. See *The Lively Experiment: The Shaping of Christianity in America* (New York: Harper & Row, 1963), pp. 108-111, and "The Theology of the Republic and the Orthodox Mind," *Journal of the American Academy of Religion* 44 (March 1976):105-113.

[8]John F. Rowe, *A History of Reformatory Movements Resulting in a Restoration of the Apostolic Church*, 5th ed. (Cincinnati, Ohio: G. W. Rice, 1884), pp. 119, v-vi, 181-82.

[9]N. B. Hardeman, *Hardeman's Tabernacle Sermons* (Nashville, Tenn.: Gospel Advocate, 1928), 3:89-92, 93-95; cf. also 5:110 (1942). On the intense biblical restorationism of the sixteenth and seventeenth-century Reformed tradition, see T. Dwight Bozeman, *To Live Ancient Lives: The Primitivist Dimension of Puritanism* (Chapel Hill, N.C.: University of North Carolina, 1988), and Allen and Hughes, *Discovering Our Roots: The Ancestry of Churches of Christ* (Abilene, Tex.: Abilene Christian University, 1988), pp. 21-48.

[10]F. J. A. Hort, *The Way, the Truth, and the Life* (New York: Macmillan, 1893), p. 91.

[11]David Steinmetz, *Memory and Mission: Theological Reflections on the Christian Past* (Nashville, Tenn.: Abingdon, 1988), pp. 28-29. For an example of such engagement with other traditions, see Allen and Hughes, *Discovering Our Roots*, esp. pp. 113-150.

[12]See Thomas H. Olbricht, "Alexander Campbell as Theologian," *Impact 21* (1988): 22-37.

[13]T. S. Eliot, *The Complete Poems and Plays, 1909-1950* (New York: Harcourt, Brace, Jovanovich, 1980), p.101.

2

The Familiar World of the Bible

...the New Testament is as perfect a constitution for the worship, discipline and government of the New Testament Church. . . as the Old Testament was for the worship, discipline and government of the Old Testament Church.

—*Thomas Campbell (1809)*

No creed but the Bible; no name but that found in His word; and no practice that [is] not as old as the New Testament.

—*N. B. Hardeman (1943)*

At this crucial juncture in our history, we among Churches of Christ face the challenge of rethinking our traditional way of reading the Bible. We face this challenge for several reasons.

First, there is the simple and observable fact that, throughout Churches of Christ, many people are questioning and sometimes rejecting the traditional doctrinal system that for several generations gave Churches of Christ their distinctive identity. Acts and the Epistles as architectural "blueprint," as a rigid "pattern," as a collection of case law—these images and the interpretive method they support are steadily declining.

Some have consciously rejected this method of interpretation and begun casting about for new ones. Many others, it seems, have not intentionally rejected the traditional method but, weary with the pugnacious, debate-all-comers attitude it nurtured, have found themselves spiritually malnourished, hungry for the things of the Spirit. And so they have quietly set it aside.

In such a situation, however, spiritual disorientation easily results. With the traditional view in decline, one becomes susceptible to theological fads, to whatever seems positive and helpful at the moment. For example, one may latch onto the latest Christian bestsellers, thereby shaping for oneself what might be called a "bestseller theology." Such works may indeed be positive and helpful. But often they are biblically shallow, shaped unduly by the spirit of the age or by theological traditions of which one has little awareness. The point is that with no theological center one remains at the mercy of whatever happens to come down the pike and catch the fancy or appear "relevant."

Behind this current situation lie other reasons why we among Churches of Christ must rethink our traditional way of reading the Bible.

(1) Most important is the fact that our traditional approach, despite its strengths, unduly reflected the rationalism of the eighteenth-century Enlightenment. It imposed upon the Bible a nineteenth-century scientific grid. This approach unwittingly distorted Scripture in significant ways and thereby subtly propagated the modern, secular spirit of self-reliance.

(2) This spirit of self-reliance today takes new, ever more secular forms among Christians. Under the relentless demands for relevance, self-enhancement, and worldly success, the Bible becomes the self-help manual *par excellence*, a book containing just the things we like to hear. This current secularizing and psychologizing of Scripture provides another compelling reason why we must rethink the role of the Bible in Christian faith.

The place to start in rethinking our way of reading the Bible is with our own heritage. For until we understand something of how we got where we are, we will not see at all clearly what corrections we might need to make. In this chapter, therefore, I look first at the genius of our forebears' approach to Scripture—its high and powerful ideals, as well as some of the tensions those ideals have produced. Second, I look at how our traditional approach to Scripture was shaped by the spirit of the age in which it arose. And third, I focus on some of the problems that emerged in this approach as time passed.

Tradition and the Freedom to Restore

Alexander Campbell, perhaps the most influential shaper of our interpretive tradition, began with a most radical approach to the Bible. "I have endeavored to read the Scriptures as though no one had read them before me," he wrote, "and I am as much on my guard against reading them today, through the medium of my own views yesterday, or a week ago, as I am against being influenced by any foreign name, authority, or system whatever."[1]

Campbell saw that a heavy traditionalism bound many Christians of his day, fostering strife, division, and closed-mindedness. And he saw how tradition bound his own views and shut out a fresh reading of Scripture. So he struggled to get free and to help others get free. In this struggle he took a radical step: he envisioned the possibility of jettisoning all tradition, all personal biases, all cultural and philosophical predilections.

Behind this struggle lay a noble goal. People needed their traditional cages rattled. They needed the sharp challenge to take a fresh look at Scripture. They still do. That ability to rattle tight little cages, to shake up settled, moribund traditions, has been the greatest strength of the Stone-Campbell heritage as it has come down to present-day Churches of Christ.

The Stone-Campbell movement, whatever else one may say about it, began as a freedom movement. It was swept along by the heady excitement of "freedom's ferment" in the early decades of American nationhood. The movement emerged between 1790 and 1815 as a loose network of Christians calling for the rejection of a Protestantism dominated by creeds and clergymen, and calling for a return to the unadorned text of the New Testament as the sole norm for belief and church order.

In Virginia in 1794 James O'Kelly and others who had followed him in breaking with the Methodists adopted a manifesto that declared in part: (1) the Holy Bible our only creed and a sufficient rule of faith and practice; (2) Christian character, or vital piety, the only test of church fellowship and membership;

and (3) the right of private judgment the privilege and duty of all. In New England in 1808 Elias Smith, moved by similar sentiments, began publishing America's first religious paper, *The Herald of Gospel Liberty*.[2]

In Kentucky in 1804 Barton Stone and four other dissidents, convinced that their presbytery had become an organ of religious bondage, published the "Last Will and Testament of the Springfield Presbytery." "We will," they wrote, "that the Synod of Kentucky examine every member, who may be suspected of having departed from the Confession of Faith, and suspend every such suspected heretic immediately; in order that the oppressed may go free and taste the sweets of gospel liberty." In what was perhaps the greatest manifesto of the movement, Thomas Campbell sounded the same theme: "Resume that precious, that dear bought liberty, wherewith Christ has made his people free; a liberty from subjection to any authority but his own, in matters of religion. Call no man father, no man master upon earth;—for one is your master, even Christ."[3]

This passion for freedom from restricting human traditions was widespread in early nineteenth-century America. Stirred by the democratic revolution of the age, the slogan "No creed but the Bible" resounded throughout many Christian groups in the new American republic.

Caught up in such a milieu, leaders throughout the Stone-Campbell movement denounced the clergy as "tyrannical oppressors" and called for the abolition of all clergy/laity distinctions. They rejected human creeds when they were imposed as tests of Christian character or when they dictated terms of Christian fellowship. They pressed relentlessly for "the inalienable right of all laymen to examine the sacred writings for themselves." People needed to be delivered, Alexander Campbell urged, from "the melancholy thraldom of relentless systems."[4]

Early leaders in the movement argued tirelessly that, in contrast to the creed-bound and coercive traditions common in early America, the primitive church was essentially democratic. Thus one person wrote in 1826 that the apostolic church displayed "equality in privileges, and mutual enjoyment of equal rights, by every member of each church." "Racoon" John Smith, a powerful preacher closely associated with Campbell, could attack the ordained clergy on the same grounds: just as Americans had learned that "a nation could exist without a king on its throne," so they should see that a church could exist "without a clergyman in the sacred desk." Such freedom, equality, and mutuality could be restored only when Christians agreed to "shake off that yoke of ecclesiastical despotism, and burst those fetters of degrading tyranny."[5]

The plea for restoration of apostolic Christianity in this way became a powerful tool of dissent and renewal. People must be allowed freedom to search the Scriptures for themselves. They must have room to change and grow. Restoration therefore must be conceived as an ongoing process. In this ideal lay part of the genius of the early Stone-Campbell movement.

The genius of the movement also lay in its emphasis on the surpassing importance of knowing the Bible's contents. Campbell's time was not a golden age when most people knew their Bibles (there has been, in fact, no such time). Martin Marty argues that, though biblical images and themes pervaded nineteenth-century American culture, actual knowledge of Scripture was very low. The Bible therefore functioned as a kind of sacred icon—it functioned religiously for the masses apart from much if any knowledge of its contents.[6]

In this situation, Campbell and other pioneers of our heritage insisted that people must not simply revere the Bible; they must learn its contents. Campbell insisted that the Bible must be opened, read, and interpreted properly. Toward this end, he attempted to give people a clear, rational method by which they could do that.

Near the heart of Campbell's approach lay the conviction that in matters of faith people should confine themselves to the "plain declarations recorded in the Bible." Scripture was a sublime collection of facts. By avoiding human speculation and confining themselves to bare scriptural facts, all people could come to understand the Bible alike. The biblical message was simple and clear, needing very little interpretation.

In this way the Bible became an open book. People began reading it for themselves, believing they could understand its message without any official interpreter or creed to guide them. In an age marked by a passion for democracy, the movement caught the imaginations of thousands and spread rapidly.

The genius of our movement's approach to Scripture, then, lay primarily in two things: (1) in the face of restricting human traditions, it stressed freedom to read Scripture afresh; and (2) in the face of widespread ignorance and uncertainty about God's will, it stressed the clarity and simplicity of Scripture.

We must see, however, that these two ideals easily clashed, giving rise to tensions and ironies. For consider: if the Bible's message consisted largely of self-evident facts, and if one could easily learn those facts, there remained little cause for further searching. As a result, one central ideal of the movement—the freedom to search and restoration as process—was subtly undercut. The spirit of free inquiry gradually diminished (even though the rhetoric of freedom often remained).

Barton Stone, above all, saw this tendency clearly. "Some among ourselves," he wrote in 1836, "were for some time zealously engaged to do away with party creeds, and are yet zealously preaching against them—but instead of a written creed of man's device, they have substituted a nondescript one, and exclude good brethren from their fellowship, because they dare believe differently from their opinions."[7]

Stone here points to the central irony that has dogged our movement since its inception: the tendency to creedalize the absence of creeds, to make non-sectarian claims a centerpiece of one's own sect, to make rejection of all human tradition a fixture in one's own robust tradition, to overpower the freedom to search with the duty to conform.

The ideals that gave birth to our movement have always been difficult to maintain. They still are. If we hope to maintain those ideals today, we must recognize that we ourselves stand in a human tradition and that we are heirs of a particular way of reading the Bible. As we saw in chapter one, a sense of historylessness often has blinded us to this fact. Our spiritual forebears often denied any complicity in human traditions, claiming to be only a people of the Book. But try as they might they could not entirely escape the influence of culture or tradition.

A noble goal underlies such efforts. But we only harbor illusions if we think that in our interpretation of the Bible we can free ourselves entirely from a mindset shaped by tradition and culture. Thinking that we can, in fact, puts us at far greater risk of letting unrecognized and distorting assumptions control our interpretation.

Despite his heroic efforts Campbell remained, in many ways, a child of his age in the way he approached the Bible. Ironically, the very notion that one could escape history and culture altogether was itself a notion given force by the history and culture of his time. Its echoes sounded across a broad spectrum of religious groups in early nineteenth-century America, not just in the Stone-Campbell movement.[8]

Furthermore, Campbell did not just read the Bible, purely and simply. He read it as a grandchild of the Puritans. He read it as a child of the European and American Enlightenment. He read it as an ardent disciple of John Locke and of the Scottish Common Sense philosophers who adapted Locke's thought. He read it assuming as a matter of course many of the new scientific, mechanistic ways of thinking about the world. Campbell was a brilliant intellectual and an intensely serious biblical scholar but he was, like all of us, a child of his time.

The Bible as a Scientific Book

Here we must look a bit further at how the modern temper shaped Campbell and the tradition of biblical interpretation that he did so much to inaugurate.

We must understand first that the Enlightenment or Age of Reason brought a profound shift in how people viewed the world and their place in it. To put it as simply as possible, we might say that in this age the cosmos was mechanized. Scientists and thinkers like Galileo, Rene Descartes, and Isaac Newton began to picture the universe as a great machine operating according to unalterable natural laws which could be expressed with great mathematical precision. The workings of the natural world thereby became more intelligible and regular, more predictable and thus more controllable. Scientific achievement exploded, giving rise to utopian visions of human progress.

Christian observers shared much of the euphoria. They stood enthralled by the prospects of controlling nature's previously mysterious forces. But for all its gifts, the Newtonian view of nature exacted a price. The price was subtle but relentless secularization. In a Newtonian world God became more distant, more impersonal. The traditional Christian belief in "special providence"—the sense of God's immediate and personal involvement in human affairs—gradually gave way to belief in impersonal natural laws. Christian people still expressed belief in "providence," but any distinction between it and the ordinary course of nature lost meaning.

In the new mechanistic worldview, as one scholar noted recently, God became "a cosmic legislator—a 'Universal Ruler,' as Newton said. He [was] no longer 'my God,' as Luther was fond of saying. . . . The sovereign Redeemer of Luther and Calvin became the sovereign Ruler of the world machine." In the emerging view, God remained Creator and First Cause but, rather than guiding creation immediately and personally, he worked only through secondary, natural causes. The natural became sharply separated from the supernatural. In this way the "modern conception of the natural world, understood as clearly distinguished from and even opposed to an impalpable spiritual world, was. . . invented."[9]

In early nineteenth-century America, a new mindset, a new way of ordering reality, resulted from the new scientific view of the natural world. One scholar calls it "analytic-technical" thinking. This new cast of mind viewed facts of nature or empirically verifiable truths as far more reliable than the supposed truths that lay beyond physical reality. It thirsted for precise knowledge, "for logically formulated, exactly specified propositions that offered a basis for accurate prediction." It harbored suspicion for whatever did not conform to the rule of computation and usefulness. In short, it held up the natural sciences, with their rigorously empirical method, as the model for all human knowing.[10]

This new mindset profoundly shaped Christian views of the Bible in nineteenth-century America. Many Christian apologists, concerned about the possible spread of unbelief, felt that they must reconcile the Bible with the new view of nature.

Otherwise, people who now thought in more precise, scientific ways about the world might cast aspersions on the Bible as an irrational or unscientific authority. So what could make more sense than adjusting the Bible so that it fit with the Newtonian universe of natural laws? Christian apologists proceeded to do just that. They modernized the Bible so that people would find it more scientific and thus more palatable. They rationalized the Bible, bending and shaping it to fit the modern temper.

This rationalization of the Bible—and thus of the Christian faith—did not occur overnight. It occurred through a long, complex, and subtle process. A few people became Deists or exponents of "natural religion," glorifying human reason and playing fast and loose with the Bible. Most believers shunned such a radical step, however, and clung to orthodoxy and to the Bible as divine revelation.

But to varying degrees many devout Christian apologists aggressively fitted the Bible to the scientific model. Entranced by the analytic-technical view of things, they "naturalized" the Bible, that is, turned it into a collection of facts analogous to the facts of nature.

The results, not surprisingly, paralleled the impact of Newtonian science on the natural world: the Bible became more mechanical, more precise, more impersonal, less mysterious, more subject to human mastery. It became less the living voice of God calling people into communion with the divine and more a collection of precise propositions subject to scientific verification. Read in this way, the Bible revealed a God who was more predictable, more attuned to the harmonies of the modern world.

By the dawn of the nineteenth century, these modernizing forces had done much to shape how American Protestants read the Bible. One can discern particularly a heightened literalism. The Protestant Reformation of the sixteenth-century had stressed the primacy of the literal meaning of Scripture, but the recasting of the Bible according to scientific models greatly heightened focus on the literal sense. Several scholars in fact have noted that by 1800 "[American] Protestants in general and Evangelicals in particular read the Bible with a flat-footed literalness unparalleled in the annals of Christianity."[11]

What does all this say about Churches of Christ and the way we traditionally have read the Bible? Simply this: our approach to the Bible was fashioned in this context. It says that our forebears did not read the Bible in a vacuum but that they read it with a mindset shaped by a particular modern world-view. We must now look briefly at how they did this.

Churches of Christ and a Scientific Bible

The first thing to say is that our early leaders, like many Protestant theologians of their day, naturalized the Bible as a scientific book of "facts." To do this they drew upon what many people of the time called the "Baconian Philosophy" (named after Francis Bacon, the seventeenth-century pioneer of the scientific method).[12]

The great appeal of Baconianism lay in the simple fact that it provided a philosophical base for applying the day's scientific methods to the Bible. Nature consists of facts, the thinking went, and so does the Bible. The natural scientist inductively gathers his facts from nature. The scriptural "scientist" inductively gathers his facts from Scripture. The natural scientist, reasoning from the facts, reaches precise and certain knowledge. The scriptural "scientist," likewise reasoning from the facts, also attains precise and certain knowledge. Both scientists use the same method because God created "two great volumes—the Book of Nature and the Book of Revelation."[13]

Alexander Campbell and his student James S. Lamar provide two prominent examples of this approach to the Bible. "If nature be a system," Campbell wrote in 1839, "religion is no less so. God is 'a God of order,' and that is the same as to say he is a God of system." Like nature, he added, the "Bible is a book of facts, not of opinions, theories, abstract generalities, nor of verbal definitions. It is a book of awful fact, grand and sublime beyond description. . . . The meaning of the Bible facts is the true biblical doctrine."

Thus Campbell could urge that the "inductive style of inquiring and reasoning is to be as rigidly carried out in reading and teaching Bible facts and documents, as in the analysis and synthesis of physical nature." In the same way that natural science, by confining itself to facts, had brought harmony and certainty, so the "divine science of religion," following the same method, would bring the same degree of precision and harmony to a divided Christendom.[14]

James Lamar, writing in 1859, pushed the analogy even further. The Bible "is a record in all respects analogous to that of a competent scientific observer," he proclaimed, "a record containing like his, rules, laws, incidents, circumstances, influences, modifications, and everything necessary to enable us to rise to the clear, full, and joyful comprehension of the truth." By using the inductive scientific method to focus exclusively on the facts, everyone will reach perfect agreement. They can "perceive the exact place and precise force of every fact, incident, precept, doctrine, and communication." They can "assign every sentence its proper place, and give to every word its legitimate force."[15]

From Campbell onward this scientifically precise way of reading the Bible held sway. In the early years of the twentieth century, an influential leader in the movement expressed the prevailing view: "Bacon's inductive method is as valuable when applied to the Bible as when applied anywhere else." Another writer put it somewhat more emphatically: "nothing more respecting the Scripture method need be said, for it is everywhere apparent that when the Lord would conduct an investigation on any subject, He did it by the inductive method."[16]

One can hardly exaggerate the significance of the Baconian inductive method, for it gave rise, a generation after Campbell, to a stringent "pattern" orthodoxy that has formed the very identity of Churches of Christ down to recent years.

Moses Lard (1818-1880), a prominent preacher and editor, played a key role in this development. Though taking his cues from Campbell's approach to the Bible, Lard was among the first to systematize and harden the "command, example, and necessary inference" schema that became the standard among Churches of Christ. Lard and numerous other second-generation leaders hardened Campbell's Baconian rationalism, pushing it to dogmatic lengths that Campbell, with his passion for unity, had resisted.

Lard's thought clearly reflects the analytic-technical mindset produced by the new scientific worldview. "In every attempt to . . . effect a reformation," Lard wrote in 1863, "the very first thing to be done is the formation of a theory approaching completeness . . . and in all the particulars exact." True restoration therefore depended, Lard asserted, on two fundamental things: first, "accepting the *exact* meaning of Holy Writ as our religious theory" and second, "the *minute conformity* of our practice to the revealed will of Christ."

By using biblical commands, examples, and necessary inferences, one constructed an exact pattern for belief and practice, a pattern in which "human elements are absolutely excluded." And the pattern allowed no deviation. One who does deviate, Lard warned, "has by the act become apostate from our ranks."[17]

For a century this way of reading the Bible remained overwhelmingly dominant. In the twentieth century, for example, this approach underlay the five series of "Tabernacle Sermons" delivered by N. B. Hardeman in Nashville (a series that, in the judgment of one historian, brought our movement to a "high water mark in its consciousness of its identity").[18]

This approach, in fact, became a powerful tradition—one held in place all the more securely by the illusion that we harbored no human traditions. A constant rhetoric of historylessness (as we saw in chapter one) hid the modern origins of the tradition. It hid from our view the fact that this way of reading the Bible was uniquely modern, that it was shaped by the new mechanistic worldview, the adulation of scientific empiricism, and the analytic-technical mindset produced in this new environment.[19]

The sharp irony is inescapable: we were a people claiming to occupy only primitive ground while holding profoundly modern assumptions about the Bible.

We should not let this irony, however, obscure the gains our spiritual forebears made with their "scientific" approach to the Bible. Faced with religious shallowness and confusion on the American frontier, they insisted on sober reflection, reasonable investigation, and objective clarity. They stressed that the Bible, because it was an objective, historically-given revelation from God, cannot mean whatever people want it to mean. So people must exert strenuous effort to downplay their feelings

and cherished traditions and, as Campbell insisted, come within
"understanding distance" of theBible. Furthermore, in an age of
democratic individualism, this approach offered an exciting
possibility: ordinary people can understand the Bible for themselves.

Problems

But if there were gains with this approach to the Bible,
there were also losses. Serious ones. As the tradition hardened
into a strict and formal orthodoxy, the problems became more
apparent.

(1) *The traditional approach elevated inorganic, impersonal,
and mechanistic models of the Bible, the church, and the Christian life.*
In this it simply reflected the Enlightened spirit of the age. Just
as scientists of the day mechanized and depersonalized the
cosmos, so theologians tended to mechanize and depersonalize
the Bible. The Bible became a kind of constitution (analogous
to the U.S. Constitution), an architectural blueprint, a legal
brief, a system of "facts." The Bible became an inert object, a
compendium of separate facts and commands rather than a
unified, personal story of God's acts and character.

This view of the Bible, in turn, shaped our traditional
formulations of the gospel and our thinking about the church.
Thus the gospel, in one of the most common traditional
formulations, consisted of "facts to be believed" (which satisfies
human intellect), "commands to be obeyed" (which challenges
human willpower), and "promises to be enjoyed" (which appeal
to human emotion).[20] Here the divine initiative, the unfathomable grace of God, the mystery of the cross, the suffering love of
the Father displayed in the sacrifice of the Son—all themes
which cluster at the heart of the gospel—recede into the
background. The focus falls instead on human understanding
and performance.

Inorganic models of the church likewise predominated.
The true church conformed perfectly to a precise blueprint, a
divine checklist. All the pieces must be in place, for any missing
element or incorrect practice invalidated it.

In general members of Churches of Christ often operated with what one might call the "balloon theory" of theology.

We all know that a balloon, inflated with air or gas, blows apart when punctured by a single pin. For a balloon cannot endure the tiniest of ruptures. In the same way, one doctrinal aberration results in the collapse of orthodoxy; one departure from the pattern, as Moses Lard put it, makes one an "apostate from our ranks."

But in fact the gospel does not consist simply of facts and commands. It does not make "minute conformity" the foundation for a person's relationship with God. Rather, it announces God's initiative towards human beings. It speaks of human sin and rebellion, of God's suffering and searching love, of divine mercy and forgiveness, of covenant faithfulness. And it calls people into a living relationship with God grounded in love, trust, and humble submission.

Campbell, on occasion, felt the need to address this issue. "It is the image of Christ the Christian looks for and loves," he wrote in 1837, "and this does not consist in being exact in a few [doctrinal] items, but in general devotion to the whole truth as far as known." He added that, if forced to choose between one who agreed with him on the "essentials" and one who did not but who was more "spiritually minded and devoted to the Lord," "I could not hesitate a moment in giving the preference of my heart to the one that loveth most."[21]

If the gospel does not consist of bare facts and commands, neither is the church an inanimate object. It is the body of Christ, a living, breathing organism, and living bodies can survive many wounds and live with many imperfections. Living bodies can contract diseases and recover, even lose body parts and remain vibrantly alive.

The focus on inorganic, mechanistic models reflected an unwitting but pronounced accommodation to modernity. And this accommodation underlay other problems.

(2) *By elevating scientific models of thinking, our traditional approach violated the historical and literary character of the Bible.* Here I must first clarify what I mean by "historical," for the word has a double meaning. Most simply it means that someone really existed or something really happened—that Moses really lived, for example, or that Jesus really rose from the dead. Our

traditional approach, to be sure, never violated the historical character of the Bible in this sense.

But the term also has a second, more subtle meaning. It means conditioned by history, shaped by a particular time and place, situated in a particular culture. When I say that our traditional approach violated the Bible's historical character, I use the term in this second sense.

By naturalizing the Bible as a body of "facts," the traditional approach atomized Scripture or broke it up into disconnected doctrinal "facts." The New Testament (or at least Acts and the Epistles) became, in practice, a field of doctrinal facts from which one could gather almost indiscriminately. Doctrinal propositions could be assembled from across the New Testament writings with little or no regard for historical context, for the author's intention, or for literary form and function. "Concordance preaching" resulted—the stringing together of texts from across the New Testament based on the appearance of a single word or phrase in the concordance.[22]

Alexander Campbell, for his part, sought to restrain this atomizing of the text by emphasizing Scripture's varying "historical circumstances." He understood well the historical distance between the biblical world and our own. In the first of his rules for interpretation, Campbell asserted that "the peculiarities of the author, the age in which he lived, his style, mode of expression, . . . date, place, and occasion [of writing], are obviously necessary to a right application of any thing in the book." Another of his rules stated that "We must come within the understanding distance. . . . All beyond that distance cannot understand God; all within it can easily understand him in all matters of piety and morality."[23]

But for many of those who came after Campbell, this concern for historical interpretation diminished or was lost. For the Baconian method which Campbell had used actually worked at cross purposes. Among Churches of Christ, the effect of the Baconian method was to shut down serious attention to Scripture's historical or cultural settings. It effectively cut the diverse biblical writings loose from their historical, cultural moorings, so that the meaning of any given text was not shaped significantly by the historical setting in which it originated.

Such an approach, in effect, collapsed the historical distance between "then" and "now," between "what it *meant*" and "what it *means*." It thereby made it all too easy to read into the Bible our modern, taken-for-granted ways of thinking. It made "common sense" the interpretive rule, failing to perceive that what is simply "common sense" in one age or culture may make little sense in another.

Besides lifting the text out of its historical settings, our traditional "scientific" approach also trod roughly over the literary forms of Scripture. It partook of the "flat-footed literalness," mentioned earlier, that arose among nineteenth-century American Protestants. Again, remember the analytic-technical mindset: it valued precise, discursive, propositional language; it devalued poetry, metaphor, image, and imagination, for they were not scientifically precise.

The shapers of our tradition read the Bible with this mindset. As a result, they reduced figurative or poetic language to propositional language. Though the Bible teems with poetry, metaphor, and parable, they most often viewed such language as mere illustration or embellishment of truths that can be stated more simply and precisely.

James Lamar put it typically—and bluntly. To find scriptural truth, he wrote, one must eliminate Scripture's "highly-colored imagery and bold hyperboles, with all that extravagance of diction which is proper to poetry," and retain only the "real facts and unadorned doctrine remaining as residual phenomena after those things are excluded." The "poetic element," in short, must be "eliminated" or "rendered simple."[24]

John Sweeney (1834-1908), another prominent second-generation preacher, explained how the New Testament itself did this. Faced with Jesus' many figures of speech, for example, one should simply turn to those texts in Acts and the Epistles which restate the point in plain, literal language. One could do this because of one important fact: "All [Jesus] meant by all his parables, and by all the figures he made use of, we have in Acts of Apostles and their Epistles to the churches, in unparabolic, or *literal* language. Absolutely *all*!" Indeed, Sweeney thought that one easily introduced doctrinal error by "going beyond the ample, literal teaching of the inspired apostles, to the uninterpreted figures, parables, and prophecies of our Lord."[25]

This view became standard in the movement. Prominent writer and preacher T. W. Brents wrote, for example, that after Pentecost "the time for figures had passed." He explained: "While the kingdom was yet in prospect, Jesus taught the people by parables and figures; but after its establishment, figures gave place to facts, commands, and promises."[26]

So poetry must be boiled down to propositional truths, Jesus' astonishing metaphors to statements of "fact," the parables to straightforward, didactic points. One must, as Fred Craddock characterized this approach, "boil the text down to a few basic truths and preach the stain in the bottom of the cup."

Such an approach, however, violates the form of the biblical material. Metaphor and image are not superfluous or expendable—we can hardly conceive or speak of God without them. Parables are not mere illustrations. Poetic language is not mere window-dressing. These literary forms are not extra verbiage embellishing some doctrinal substance. "The literary genres of the Bible," Paul Ricoeur insists, "do not constitute a rhetorical facade to pull down in order to reveal some thought content that is indifferent to its literary vehicle."[27] Rather, form and content are deeply intertwined. Scripture's imaginative language opens up dimensions of divine truth to us that "factual" language cannot open up. But more of this in the next chapter.

(3) *Our traditional way of reading the Bible has restricted our spiritual resources for dealing with the advanced secularization of our time.* Again, remember the spirit of the age in which our movement emerged: enormous confidence in human reason and technique; a growing sense of human autonomy; a sense that God was not directly involved in sustaining the world and in directing human affairs.

Imbibing this spirit to some degree, we read the Bible more with an eye for the human initiative than for the divine. God had finished his part long ago (when he revealed the Bible) and now it was all up to human beings to do their part. Divine providence became nearly indistinguishable from the fixed course of nature, the Holy Spirit nearly indistinguishable from the Bible. One's spiritual standing depended on mastery of a precise body of doctrinal "facts."

Meanwhile the secularizing forces unleashed in the Enlightenment became ever more dominant. The analytic-technical mindset carried the day. It made stupendous promises—and it delivered. Human beings could master their environment. They could better human life. They could shoot for the moon—and they did. With stunning successes one right after another. Glory to man in the highest!

But there was a catch. The scientific mindset possessed a marvelous ability to explain and control the natural world but made little progress in explaining and controlling the human spirit or self. Technology dazzled the mind with a rush of comforts, conveniences, and cures; but alienation, global violence, despair, and suicide seemed to keep pace. Success in answering the "How?" questions far outran the "Whys?" Newton's mechanized cosmos was proving insufficient to nurture the human spirit.

The result in our time is a decline of the Enlightenment worldview—some would even say its death. The prestige of scientific empiricism is seriously waning. Suspicion of technological advancement abounds. We witness around us the decay of jaunty Enlightenment rationalism, for many people sense that it has imperiled the human soul.[28]

With this decay of the Enlightenment worldview, we reach an advanced stage of secularization. In this advanced stage the Enlightenment's soaring confidence in human reason and achievement degenerates into an "isolating preoccupation with the self." A sense of transcendent moral values fades, so that the self must choose or create its own values. Objective moral goodness clearly revealed in nature's laws "turns into the subjective goodness of getting what you want and enjoying it. Utility replaces duty; self-expression unseats authority. 'Being good' becomes 'feeling good.'" In such a situation "no autonomous standard of good and evil survives outside the needs of individual psyches for growth."[29]

Religion prospers in this deeply secularized environment. But, as we see most crassly in the New Age Movement, it becomes narcissistic, eclectic, and trendy. People value religion to the extent that it enhances and fulfills the self. They dabble in this, that, and the other, judging all of it by how well it works and how it makes them feel. The Bible gets the same treatment. People find in it what they want to find or "need" to find. The Bible becomes a therapeutic book wonderfully designed to enhance the self, not so much a holy book through which God seeks to subvert and powerfully transform the self.[30]

Now, with this advanced secularism of our time, Churches of Christ find themselves in a difficult situation. The decline of the Enlightenment worldview with its scientific mode of knowing has meant a corresponding decline of our traditional approach to the Bible (which was, to a significant degree, rooted in that worldview). Members of Churches of Christ today, in growing numbers, simply reflect the shifting cultural mindset. The traditional approach to Scripture may not be consciously discarded. But it loses cogency and recedes.

But the problem is not simply a matter of cultural change. It is also that the traditional approach, because it fostered a kind of spiritual self-reliance, proves theologically inadequate to address an individualistic, self-indulgent, highly-secularized age. How, we might ask, can a self-help Christianity direct increasingly self-indulgent people away from self?

Conclusion

We have traced in broad strokes our traditional approach to the Bible. Several things stand out. First, we indeed have a traditional approach, and it is rooted in the progressive thought-world of early nineteenth-century America. Second, this approach brought both gains and losses. It stressed the reasonableness of Scripture and brought clarity in the midst of confusion. But in the process it also made concessions to the secular spirit of the age that were to prove damaging. Third, we now face the challenge of reading the Bible afresh, in light of past gains and losses.

But something else must be said. Though we have looked to the past with a critical eye, we must never forget this: that Scripture is able to overide the interpretive rules and systems we construct for it; that God works through and beyond our limited, time-bound ways of reading his Word to draw people with searching hearts into relationship with him. This God did with our spiritual forebears. This God does with us today. The divine Word breaks out of the constraints we place upon it. Through it God graciously uplifts and transforms those who humbly seek.

With the past and its somewhat familiar contours in view, I turn in the next chapter to four areas where we might find corrective and fresh perspective in our reading of Scripture today.

Notes

Epigraphs: Thomas Campbell, *The Declaration and Address of the Christian Association of Washington* (Washington, Pa., 1809), p. 16; N. B. Hardeman, *Tabernacle Sermons* (Nashville, Tenn.: Gospel Advocate, 1943), 5:111.

[1]Alexander Campbell, *Christian Baptist* (April 3, 1826):229.

[2]Leonard Allen, "James O'Kelly and the 'Five Cardinal Principles of the Christian Church'," *Christian Standard* 114 (August 5, 1979):708-709; and Nathan O. Hatch, "Elias Smith and the Rise of Religious Journalism in the Early Republic," in *Printing and Society in Early America*, ed. William L. Joyce, et. al. (Worcester, Mass.: American Antiquarian Society, 1983), pp. 250-77.

[3]Charles A. Young, *Historical Documents Advocating Christian Union* (Chicago, Ill.: Christian Century, 1904), pp. 19-26; Campbell, *Declaration and Address*, pp. 14-15.

[4]Alexander Campbell, *Christian Baptist* 3 (January 2, 1826):209, and ibid. (April 3, 1826):229.

[5]John Smith, *Christian Messenger* 1 (November 1829):22; T. M. Allen, *Christian Messenger* 1 (March 24, 1829):110.

[6]Martin Marty, "America's Iconic Book," in *Humanizing America's Iconic Book*, ed. Gene M. Tucker and Douglas A. Knight (Chico, Calif.: Scholar's Press, 1980), pp. 1-23.

[7]Barton Stone, "Desultory Remarks," *Christian Messenger* 10 (December 1836):182.

[8]See Nathan O. Hatch, "*Sola Scriptura* and *Novus Ordo Seclorum*," in *The Bible in America: Essays in Cultural History*, ed. Nathan O. Hatch and Mark A. Noll (New York: Oxford University, 1982), pp. 59-78.

[9]Gary B. Deason, "Reformation Theology and the Mechanistic Conception of Nature," in *God and Nature: Historical Essays on the Encounter between Christianity and Science*, ed. David C. Lindberg and Ronald L. Numbers (Berkeley, Calif.: University of California, 1986), p. 187; James Turner, *Without God, Without Creed: The Origins of Unbelief in America* (Baltimore, Md.: Johns Hopkins University, 1985), p. 38. See also Richard S. Westfall, "The Rise of Science and the Decline of Orthodox Christianity: A Study of Kepler, Descartes, and Newton," in *God and Nature*, pp. 218-37.

[10]Turner, *Without God, Without Creed*, pp. 132-40.

[11]Ibid., p. 144; Hans Frei, *The Eclipse of Biblical Narrative: A Study in Eighteenth and Nineteenth Century Hermeneutics* (New Haven, Conn.: Yale University, 1974), pp. 18-41, 55-56.

[12]For an indepth treatment of Baconianism in American religion, see T. Dwight Bozeman, *Protestants in an Age of Science: The Baconian Ideal in Antebellum American Protestant Thought* (Chapel Hill, N.C.: University of North Carolina, 1977), and George M. Marsden, "Everyone One's Own Interpreter? The Bible, Science, and Authority in Mid-Nineteenth-Century America," in *The Bible in America*, pp. 79-100.

[13]James S. Lamar, *The Organon of Scripture: Or, the Inductive Method of Biblical Interpretation* (Philadelphia, Pa., 1859), pp. 187-91. For a survey of the long history of the "two books" idea, see Roland M. Frye, "The Two Books of God," *Theology Today* 39 (1982):260-66.

[14]Alexander Campbell, *The Christian System* (Bethany, VA, 1839), pp. 2, 6; Campbell, "Schools and Colleges—No. 2," *Millennial Harbinger* (March 1850):172; and "Principles of Interpretation," in *A Connected View of the Principles and Rules by Which the Living Oracles May Be Intelligently and Certainly Interpreted* (Bethany, Va., 1835), pp. 13-99.

[15]Lamar, *Organon of Scripture*, pp. 193, 196, 197. See C. Leonard Allen, "Baconianism and the Bible in the Disciples of Christ: James S. Lamar and *The Organon of Scripture*," *Church History* 55 (March 1986):65-80; Thomas H. Olbricht, "The Rationalism of the Restoration," *Restoration Quarterly* 11 (Second Quarter 1968):77-88; and Michael Casey, "The Origins of the Hermeneutics of the Churches of Christ: Part Two, The Philosophical Background," *Restoration Quarterly 31* (Fourth Quarter 1989).

[16]Z. T. Sweeney, introduction to Isaac Errett, *Bible Readings* (Cincinnati, Ohio: Standard, 1913), p. vii; David R. Dungan, *Hermeneutics: A Text Book* (Cincinnati, Ohio, 1888), p. 101.

[17]Moses Lard, "The Reformation for Which We Plead—What Is It?" *Lard's Quarterly* 1 (1863):14,22; Lard, "Instrumental Music in Churches and Dancing," ibid., p. 331. For indepth treatment of this shift, see Michael Casey, "The Development of Necessary Inference in the Hermeneutics of the Disciples of Christ/Churches of Christ" (Ph.D. diss., University of Pittsburgh, 1985), especially pp. 370ff, and Russ Dudrey, "Restorationist Hermeneutics Among Churches of Christ: Why Are We at an Impasse?" *Restoration Quarterly* 30 (First Quarter 1988):24-36.

[18]N. B. Hardeman, *Hardeman's Tabernacle Sermons* (Nashville, Tenn.: Gospel Advocate, 1938), 4:52-59; William Woodson, *Standing for Their Faith: A History of Churches of Christ in Tennessee, 1900-1950* (Henderson, Tenn.: J & W Publications, 1979), p. 74.

[19]George Marsden concludes that nineteenth and early twentieth century Protestant evangelicalism was "early modern" in its assumptions and structures of thought as opposed to "late modern." See his essay, "Evangelicals, History, and Modernity," in *Evangelicalism and Modern America*, ed. George Marsden (Grand Rapids, Mich.: Eerdmans, 1984), p. 98. The same can be said for Churches of Christ taken as a movement.

[20]Jesse L. Sewell, "The Gospel," in *Life and Sermons of Jesse L. Sewell*, by David Lipscomb (Nashville, Tenn.: Gospel Advocate, 1891), pp. 174-75; John F. Rowe, *A History of Reformatory Movements Resulting in a Restoration of the Apostolic Church* (Cincinnatti, Ohio, 1884), pp. 182-83; Isaac Errett, *Bible Readings* (Cincinnati, Ohio: Standard, 1913), 1:182-86; and N. B. Hardeman, *Tabernacle Sermons* (1923, 1938), 2:92-95; 4:68-70. Hardeman explained that there are "three facts—the death, the burial, and the resurrection of Christ; three commandments—faith in the Lord Jesus Christ, genuine repentance of all our sins, and burial with him upon a confession of faith...; [and] three splendid promises—namely, the forgiveness of all of our sins, the reception of the Holy Spirit, the hope of everlasting bliss" (2:94).

[21]Alexander Campbell, "Any Christians Among Protestant Parties," *Millennial Harbinger*, 1, new series (September 1837):412. Cf. Campbell, "To an Independent Baptist," *Christian Baptist* 3 (May 1, 1826):200-205.

[22]Fred Craddock speaks of being "seduced by the concordance." See his discussion in *The Bible in the Pulpit of the Christian Church*, 1981 Forrest

F. Reed Lectures (Claremont, Calif.: Disciples Seminary Foundation, 1982), pp. 19-23.

[23]Campbell, *Christian System*, pp. 3-5. See also Eugene Boring, "The Formation of a Tradition: Alexander Campbell and the New Testament," *Disciples Theological Digest* 2 (1987):22-23.

[24]Lamar, *Organon of Scripture*, p. 235.

[25]John Sweeney, *Sweeney's Sermons* (Nashville, Tenn.: Gospel Advocate, 1892), pp. 121-22. On Sweeney, see Bill Love, "The Preaching of John Sweeney (1834-1908): A Case Study in Restoration Hermeneutic," *Restoration Quarterly* 31 (First Quarter 1989):27-37.

[26]T. W. Brents, *The Gospel Plan of Salvation*, 12th ed. (Nashville, Tenn.: Gospel Advocate, 1928), pp. 208, 207.

[27]Paul Ricoeur, "Toward a Hermeneutic of the Idea of Revelation," in *Essays on Biblical Interpretation*, ed. Lewis S. Mudge (Philadelphia, Pa.: Fortress, 1980), p. 91.

[28]See Langdon Gilkey, *Society and the Sacred: Toward a Theology of Culture in Decline* (New York: Crossroad, 1981), p. 3-14, and William Barrett, *Death of the Soul: From Descartes to the Computer* (Garden City, N.Y.: Anchor/Doubleday, 1986).

[29]Robert Bellah, et. al., *Habits of the Heart: Individualism and Committment in American Life* (New York: Harper & Row, 1986), pp. 56, 77, 232.

[30]For a fuller treatment of secularized religion, see Allen, Hughes, and Weed, *The Worldly Church: A Call for Biblical Renewal* (Abilene, Tex.: Abilene Christian University, 1988), chapter 2.

3

The Strange World of the Bible

We have heard the fact, let us seek the mystery.
—*Augustine of Hippo (416)*

The [biblical] poets want us to re-experience the present world under a different set of metaphors, and they want us to entertain an alternative world not yet visible.
—*Walter Brueggemann (1987)*

Exploring a Strange World

If the modern rationalization of the Bible as a scientific book made the Bible comfortably familiar and nicely attuned to modern Western thought, we must rediscover its strangeness. By this I mean two things. First, I mean that the Bible is a collection of writings rooted deeply in a world that is remote to us. It reflects languages, cultures, and world views as strange to us as those of rural Kenya or Kurdistan. Only as we realize that we are outsiders can we enter that strange world and to some degree become insiders.

Second, I mean that even for insiders the Bible retains a kind of strangeness, for it reveals a God who works in strange and surprising ways. The God of Scripture time and again shatters conventional views of the possible and the impossible. God breaks open new, often unimagined vistas, bestows hope where none remains, does impossible things with impossible people. Strange indeed.

Rediscovering the strangeness of the Bible, I suggest, will help us resist the secular spirit that shapes Churches of Christ so powerfully today. In the first place, if the biblical writings are rooted deeply in a remote world, that means we will have to use careful thought, patient study, and the tools of historical investigation to open it up. The Bible cannot mean what we, pouring intently over our private want list, might like for it to mean. Rooted in history, the Bible has fixed points that control our interpretation.

In the second place, the awareness that God works in unexpected and surprising ways means that we cannot lock the Scriptures into our own rational system. We cannot finally control them. We cannot master holy things in the way that science has sought to master worldly things.

I turn now to look further at these two aspects of the Bible's strangeness.

First, Scripture reflects a world that in many ways is strange and remote to us. Scripture reflects, in fact, the mores, idioms, and thought patterns of at least five distinct cultures: Bronze Age, Iron Age, Persian, Hellenistic, and Roman. Good interpretation of Scripture therefore demands that one first recognize and then seek to enter those strange and distant cultures. It demands, in other words, that one become involved to some degree in a cross-cultural enterprise.

Entering a strange culture is always a challenging and somewhat disorienting experience. One finds that things are often not what they at first appear to be, and that one's own long-assumed framework of meaning cannot be counted on to make sense of things.

Consider, for example, a person who moves from America to live among the Kipsigis people of Kenya.[1] The newcomer immediately faces, in addition to the strange sounding language, many other puzzling things. He notices that men hold hands with men but greet their wives (even after a long absence) with a mere handshake. He hears that church starts at 10 AM, but when he arrives on time, hardly anyone is present. People slowly trickle in. Finally around 11 AM someone says it is time to begin the meeting. They sing many songs. Two or three men preach long sermons. No one seems to take much account of time, and the service finally breaks up about 2 or 3 PM.

As time passes our newcomer finds that things are strange in much more subtle and profound ways. He passes an old woman on the road one day and hears her greet a young boy with the words, "How are you, grandfather?" Puzzled, our newcomer turns to his guide, who tells him about the Kipsigis' *Kuurenet* or calling rite. He explains that when a child is born old matriarchs gather around and ask, "Tell us, young child, who you are?" The child sneezes or coughs at some point and the women find their answer; they learn which of their ancestors has been reborn.

Our newcomer learns that, in contrast to America where people often view sexual offenses as the most scandalous and weighty, the Kipsigis view anger as the most weighty and disturbing offense. Anger is not simply an emotional outburst that can be easily brushed aside and forgotten but rather an evil power almost bewitching in its force.

Because our newcomer to Kenya faces strange things at every turn, he must become a patient asker of questions. It is not simply that he faces a strange language and odd customs—that would be challenging enough—but that he faces a different worldview (or cosmology). Thus he must not jump quickly to conclusions; rather, he must set aside many of his own cultural assumptions about how things work and what they mean. If he hopes to understand the culture accurately, then he must become a diligent interpreter of life in that culture.

The modern person who approaches Scripture faces an analogous situation. She too must become a diligent interpreter, for she faces a "geographical, linguistic, psychological, cosmological and chronological gulf between the ancient Near East and modern America."[2] By failing to recognize that gulf, that strangeness, she easily modernizes the text, reading into it what to her seems only natural, logical, and common sensical.

It is precisely this tendency that our traditional way of reading the Bible has fostered. As we saw in chapter two, the adoption of Common Sense, scientific ways of thinking tended to cut the biblical text loose from its cultural context, thus collapsing the distance between "then" and "now." The strangeness was removed—and with it the need for serious historical interpretation. One simply collected biblical "facts" and arranged them into patterns, for the Bible said what it meant and meant what it said. Or so it seemed.

We can see this process at work in Alexander Campbell's understanding of the biblical metaphor of the Kingdom of God, a metaphor which is central to his entire theology. Using the analogy of human kingdoms and influenced by the "social compact" theory of the philosopher John Locke, Campbell saw the Kingdom of God as composed of five elements: the constitution, the king, the subjects, the territory, and the laws. The constitution was the plan of salvation conceived by God before time began (and reflected in the New Testament). The king or "constitutional monarch" was Jesus Christ, whose reign began on the first Pentecost after his ascension. The subjects were all those who had been born again. The territory was the "whole earth." And the Kingdom's laws were found in the New Testament (primarily in Acts and the Epistles), for the king made his apostles the legislators of the Kingdom.

This way of interpreting the biblical metaphor of the Kingdom of God did much to shape the way Campbell (and his heirs) viewed the New Testament. The New Testament became basically "the statute-book of Heaven," a uniform legal code for the church (which was virtually equated with the Kingdom). Campbell himself was not entirely comfortable with such a view, and some tension on this issue appears in his writing, but the logic of his kingdom theory pushed him in that direction. Among many of his heirs the legal metaphor became dominant. The New Testament became primarily a book of case law.[3]

The point here is that Campbell, for all his concern for coming within "understanding distance" of Scripture, interpreted the biblical metaphor of the Kingdom of God through a foreign lens. He drew upon a modern, western "social compact" theory widely held in the political thought of his own day. He thereby lost the strangeness of this prominent biblical metaphor. He lost something of its expansive, open-ended, dynamic dimension. This rich metaphor finds it proper meaning against the backdrop of the Jewish Scriptures and early Judaism (especially the apocalyptic tradition), not in early modern political theory.[4]

At this juncture in our history, we must make or renew a commitment to historical interpretation (or historical criticism), that is, to the task of placing the biblical writings squarely in their original historical, religious, and literary environment. As Edgar Krentz put it, historical interpretation

> puts us in the place of Jesus' first hearers by making the Bible seem *strange* and *foreign*. Palestine is an earthy place; Israel's prophets and Jesus do not resemble the well-laundered pictures of them prevalent in much piety and art. Historical criticism makes the gap between us and the biblical world as wide as it actually is, forces us to face the peculiarity and particularity of the texts in their world, and confronts us with the Jesus who is the challenge to all cultures and securities of our world.[5]

Such a task requires patience, dedication, and an adventuresome spirit. But for a people who, throughout their history, have warned against imposing foreign ideas on the text and rallied around the cry "Back to the Bible," such a task seems wonderfully congenial and highly desirable. For historical interpretation, as Krister Stendahl suggests, (1) "guards against apologetic softenings and harmonizations, against conscious and unconscious modernizations in the interest of making the Bible more acceptable ... [to the] contemporary reader" and (2) fosters "great respect for the diversity within Scripture."[6]

So through historical interpretation we must seek to become insiders in the distant world of the Bible. We must work diligently to bridge the gulf and imaginatively enter that strange world.

But there is another dimension of the Bible's strangeness, a dimension not exhausted by historical virtuosity. We may learn the biblical languages, and that would be excellent. We may walk the terrain of Palestine, learning it sites, getting an intimate feel of the place. And that's extremely helpful. We may explore the rich worlds of Semitic, Hellenistic, and Roman culture. And that's important. All of this helps us immensely, for through it we may become somewhat of an insider in that strange world.

But another kind of strangeness remains: the strange, and strangely wonderful, ways of a transcendent God. It is this strangeness that we must not—that we finally cannot—dispel.

Yet, as we saw in the previous chapter, the modern scientific model for understanding reality drives out mystery and strangeness. It proceeds on the assumption that we can progressively shrink the mystery, pile our knowledge ever higher, and thus exercise ever greater control over our world. The scientist Lewis Thomas, though acknowledging a "wilderness of mystery" before us, put the conventional assumption plainly: "I cannot imagine any sorts of questions to be asked about ourselves or about nature that cannot sooner or later be answered, given enough time."[7]

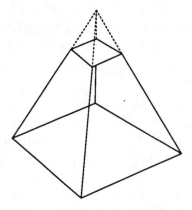

An unfinished pyramid well represents this mindset. The solid lines represent the known, the dotted lines the unknown. As knowledge mounts, the unknown, the mysterious, the strange, diminishes. Awe turns into a kind of pragmatic curiosity. The goal, ultimately, is capping off the pyramid. Such a mindset—by closing off, reducing, and controlling—propels the secularization of our time.

But there is another, very different model for understanding reality, one that confronts mystery and strangeness without driving it out. We can represent it simply by inverting our pyramid. Here the lines of understanding do not narrow and converge to a single, fixed point. Rather, they open out ever wider, reaching always beyond our grasp or control. The more we learn the more we see what there is to learn. The more we grasp the more we perceive what we do not yet grasp.[8]

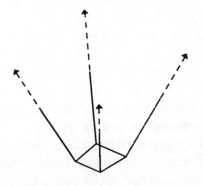

The first model reduces the sense of mystery or transcendent reality. The second enlarges it. The first diminishes awe before the strange and unknown. The second overwhelms one with it.

These models can help us rediscover the irreducible strangeness or otherness of the God whom the Bible reveals to us. But such rediscovery remains an uphill struggle. For the secular spirit of our age, with its exaltation of technique, its drive to master and control, teaches us to solve problems, not engage mystery. We live in a problem-solving world. One defines a problem, applies his or her ingenuity to it, solves it, then moves on to other problems.

As we all know by now this approach, with its technological mastery, solved many problems. Bacteria was a problem: penicillin and a host of other antibiotics solved it. Travel was a problem: steamships, then railroads, then automobiles and airplanes solved it. Long distance communication was a problem: the telegraph, then the telephone, then television, then satellites solved it.

The successes were stunning, so stunning in fact that rational, technical problem-solving became the model for all human knowing. Problem-solving meant mastery, power, and success. Who could question it? Who could top it?

Modern people that we are, we easily bring the same mindset to the Bible, and with good cause. For the Bible clearly presents us many problems to solve, many puzzles to assemble.

Who wrote Hebrews? Is Mark 16:9-20 a later addition? Why does Matthew 27:9 apparently attribute a prophecy from Zechariah to Jeremiah? What about the numbers in Numbers? What was Behemoth and Leviathan? Ad infinitum.

Modern biblical studies have shed great light on many problems and we are enriched by it. But the disposition to reduce every unknown to a potentially solvable problem misses something central about the Scriptures. It reflects the uniquely modern assumption that all reality lies open to the power of clear thought. It reduces mysteries to problems.

But Scripture does far more than present problems to be solved. It confronts us with the transcendent, the mysterious, the sacred. Think about the difference between a problem and a mystery. Simply put, we solve a problem, or at least like to think we can. And once we solve it, we can dismiss it, dispose of it. It need not concern us further, unless of course the problem proves more complex than we first thought, which then means figuring out a more intricate solution.

But a mystery is different. We do not solve true mysteries. We engage them—or rather they engage us. We participate in them. We get caught up in them. We get enticed and seized by them. "Mystery does not present itself to us as a datum of which there might be complete, 'objective' knowledge; rather mystery questions us, demands of us a response, challenges us to decide what we are to do, what we are to make of our lives."[9]

In the tradition of Churches of Christ, we have not often thought of mystery this way. Though we have occasionally acknowledged the presence of mystery, for the most part we have been extremely uncomfortable with anything that we could not solve, explain, or put in a chart. As one preacher put it, "In all places in the Scriptures where anything is spoken of as having been a mystery, it is spoken of as now made known. There is nothing spoken of as having been left a mystery now."[10] God's will may have once been a mystery hidden throughout the ages but now, with the completed New Testament, the mystery has been banished.

In scriptural usage, however, "mystery" has a double sense: it often refers to the *quantity* of the unknown (that is, to what has not yet been revealed), yet it also refers to the *quality* of the known (that is, to what has been revealed but cannot be fathomed). Facing mystery, in the first sense, means simply remaining in ignorance; facing mystery, in the second sense, means being filled with awe and wonder.

In the Ephesian letter we find both senses of the word. Ephesians 3:2-6 says that God's plan to make the Gentiles fellow heirs with Israel was a mystery. It was part of the quantity of the unknown. But what was once a mystery remains so no longer, for it has been "made known by revelation" (3:2-6; cf. Col. 1:26).

But in Ephesians 5:21-33 mystery also refers to the quality of the known. For here the writer speaks of marriage as a mystery (5:32). To a child the union between a man and a woman is a great mystery—the child simply does not know what transpires there. When the child grows up and gets married, however, we might say that in one sense the mystery is revealed. But the mystery in marriage is not thereby dispelled. For the married person discovers that the mystery in marriage was not simply a certain quantity of the unknown which, when one marries, suddenly dissipates. Rather, one finds in marriage an even deeper mystery residing in the quality or depth of the known.

So it is, the Ephesian writer says, with Christ and the church. For this relationship too is a "great mystery." To those outside the community of faith, of course, this relationship remains a mystery, an unknown. But for those who come to know it or share in it, the mystery is not thereby dispelled. For the believer discovers that the mystery in this relationship is not simply a certain quantity of the unknown which, when one enters into it, suddenly dissipates. Rather, the believer finds in Christ an ever deeper mystery residing in the dazzling quality of the known.

We might think of Scripture in a similar way. The Bible, in the final analysis, does not present a set of problems we must solve but rather a profound mystery that engages us. It holds before us the central and ultimate mystery of God. The Bible opens up that mystery to us by recounting God's loving and mighty acts in history. Thus at one level the mystery has been revealed. Yet at the same time, paradoxically, the mystery deepens as we experience the divine love and glimpse the transcendent purpose those acts reveal. Thus we are led to exclaim with the New Testament writer (who refers particularly to the incarnation): "Great beyond all question is the mystery of our religion" (1 Tim. 3:16, NEB).

We seek to probe the mystery, to be sure, thus we never devalue the life of the mind, vigorous Bible study, or the reasonableness that so satisfies and compels us. But the deeper we enter into the mystery the more it beckens and allures, dazzles and surprises. Before it we find ourselves alternately befuddled and enlightened, humbled and exhilarated. Just when we have established the boundaries of the possible, God unexpectedly enlarges them. Just when, after much patient labor, we solve a problem, we find that the solution itself thrusts us further into the divine mystery. We find, as a noted biblical scholar once exclaimed, that we may "bury ourselves in a lexicon and arise in the presence of God."[11]

A first step, then, towards a fresh perspective on Scripture involves rediscovering the strangeness of its world and of the God it reveals.

Enlarging Our Canon

A second step towards a fresh engagement with Scripture involves enlarging our canon. By that I do not mean adding new books to the Bible or seeking newly-revealed Scriptures. I mean rather taking the whole Bible with a new seriousness. I mean recovering the Jewish Scriptures as a vital and functional part of our Christian life. I mean elevating the Gospel accounts to equal status with the Epistles as authoritative documents for the church.

Here we must again look briefly at our traditional way of reading the Bible. Alexander Campbell, again, played a key role. Influenced by the covenant theology of the Reformed tradition in which he was nurtured, Campbell divided the Bible into three dispensations: the patriarchal, spanning from Adam to Moses; the Mosaic, spanning from Moses at Sinai to Peter on Pentecost; and the Christian, beginning at Pentecost and ending with the final judgment. This dispensational schema, in effect, divided the Bible into three blocks: (1) Genesis 1 through Exodus 19; (2) Exodus 20 through Acts 1; and (3) Acts 2 through Revelation 22.

On this basis Campbell stressed time and again that only biblical texts reflecting the Christian age (Acts 2 through Revelation 22) can authorize Christian faith and practice. In his famous "Sermon on the Law" he argued that because Christians do not live under the Mosaic covenant they are not bound by its laws and institutions. Rather, "[Christ's] will published in the New Testament is the sole law of the church."[12]

By dividing the Bible up this way, Campbell did not mean to disparage or jettison the Old Testament. In fact, he acknowledged that the Old Testament contained "not only much useful history and prophecy, but also many communications from God to men of immense importance to us Christians."[13] He stressed that the Old Testament contains many eternally valid teachings about God and human beings. But his emphasis fell heavily, not on those eternally valid teachings, but on the change of covenants, on Acts to Revelation as the "sole law of the church." He focused on the church's forms, structures, and ordinances, for he sought Christian unity and these issues, he judged, proved most divisive in his day.

The upshot of this focus was that Campbell operated with a well-defined canon-within-a-canon. It consisted of Acts 2-28, the Pauline Epistles, and Hebrews (which Campbell attributed to Paul). Furthermore, within Campbell's canon-within-a-canon, the book of Hebrews appears to have served as the functional center. Campbell was drawn to Hebrews, particularly to its emphasis on the change of covenants and on Old Testament events and institutions as "types" of New Testament events and institutions. Hebrews, we may conclude, provided the framework in which he interpreted Romans and the other Pauline epistles.[14]

We must see something important here. In Campbell's dispensational arrangement the Gospels and Acts 1 fall into the Mosaic dispensation. The Gospels, as a result, serve a preparatory role. Like the Old Testament, they serve primarily as preparation for the change of covenants that occurred on Pentecost. The Gospels could not provide the "laws" for

Christ's Kingdom, for the laws of a kingdom could be set forth only after that kingdom had been established. Thus Campbell wrote that the "laws and usages of the Apostles must be learned from what the Apostles published to the world, after the ascension and coronation of the King, as they are recorded in Acts of the Apostles and Epistles." One should not seek these laws, he added, "antecedent to the day of Pentecost; except so far as our Lord himself, during his lifetime, propounded the doctrine of his reign."[15]

As this last phrase indicates, Campbell did not simply lump the Gospels together with the Old Testament; however these texts clearly occupy a place of secondary importance. In this view one living under the Christian dispensation used the Gospels, particularly the miracle stories, to prove the supernatural fact of Jesus' messiahship. But once that purpose was achieved and thus the ground for faith established, the Gospels took a back seat to Acts of the Apostles and the Epistles.

Campbell's view of the Kingdom, in fact, leads to a striking conclusion: the actions of Jesus before Pentecost do not possess the same authority for the church as do the actions of the apostles after Pentecost. Jesus' life and teachings predate the establishment of the Kingdom and thus belong in the "old Jewish dispensation." For this reason Campbell and other nineteenth-century restorers believed, for example, that Christians should not use the Lord's Prayer (a prohibition that has continued among many twentieth-century Churches of Christ). The Gospels, in short, play a somewhat minimal role when it comes to preaching the gospel or instructing the church about its life together in Christ.

Such a view, however, is simply untenable, for it does not take into account the origin and purposes of the Gospel documents. The Gospels are not pre-Christian or pre-Pentecost documents at all. Far from it. Rather, the four Gospels were written to instruct and nurture specific Christian communities as they struggled with discipleship in the decades after Christ. Each Gospel writer drew selectively upon the rich tradition of stories about Jesus, shaping his message according to the needs of a particular community of Christians.[16]

Far from serving merely as preparatory documents for the Christian dispensation, the four Gospels occupy center-stage for Christians. They proclaim the gospel of Christ (just as their name suggests). They instruct the church, the community that gathers around Christ. They awaken people to the blessings and demands of life in God's kingdom. They enable us to be a Christ-centered people. By enlarging our canon, therefore, I mean restoring the Gospels to centerstage in the life of the church today.

But we must go further. We must also reclaim the Jewish Scriptures as a basic and vital part of Christian Scripture. Despite Campbell's professed regard for the Old Testament, his overall influence contributed to serious neglect of it by his heirs. Those who followed hardened Campbell's dispensational schema. Subtleties were lost. Impersonal, mechanical models of covenant obliterated vital and complex links between the testaments. The basic theology of the Old Testament, which frames and undergirds the New Testament in profound ways, faded from view. It exaggerates only a bit to say that the Old Testament—and to some degree the Gospels—dropped out of the theology of Churches of Christ.[17]

This development struck me again just recently as I looked through a widely-used Bible correspondence course. There it was, emblazoned as a subheading in one lesson—"Old Testament Removed." Of course I knew some of the distinctions it was trying to make: Christians do not observe the Mosaic covenant's religious system; they are free from Mosaic ritual and regulation (Gal. 3:1-18; Rom. 7:1-7); the written code (or letter) kills but the Spirit gives life (2 Cor. 3:6-18); Jesus abolished the "law of commandments" contained in the Old Testament (Eph. 2:11-18); the new covenant far surpasses the old in splendor (Heb. 7:1-10:18).[18]

These are significant New Testament distinctions, to be sure. But they are far more complex than the simple declaration, "Old Testament Removed," indicates. Such a declaration leaves a far different impression. It suggests that the Old Testament may be relegated safely to the background. It leaves the impression that the New Testament is theologically self-contained. And that leads to serious distortions.

We must not forget a striking fact: the Old Testament served as "the Bible" of the earliest Christians. They preached Christ from it (Acts 8:27-35). They instructed people in salvation from it. Paul had the Old Testament in mind when he wrote these words to Timothy: "From childhood you have been acquainted with the sacred writings which are able to instruct you for salvation through faith in Christ Jesus. All scripture is inspired by God and profitable for teaching, for reproof, for correction, and for training in righteousness, that the man of God may be complete, equipped for every good work" (2 Tim. 3:15-17).

Christian writings emerged gradually over a period of many years, supplementing and interpreting the Jewish Scriptures in light of Christ's coming. A New Testament canon very slowly took shape. (Only by the mid-second century A.D. do we find evidence for a collection of writings somewhat approximating our complete collection of Gospels, Acts, Epistles, and Revelation. Canonical lists containing exactly the twenty-seven books we accept today appeared only by the fourth century, though even then there was not unanimity among the various Christian communities.[19]) Throughout this period the Hebrew Scriptures remained a most basic and vital part of the Christian canon. The church always vigorously opposed those, like Marcion in the second century, who sought to ignore or remove them.

The Hebrew Scriptures remained vital because its basic theology provides the framework for all the Christian writings that eventually formed our New Testament.[20] It puts securely in place the great pillar truths on which biblical faith rests. With its revelation of God and its doctrines of creation, human being, and sin, it lays the indispensable foundation for a Christian worldview. It reveals God as creator and as the one who actively sustains the world and human life in it (Gen. 1-2; Ps. 89:9; Neh. 9:6). It makes a sharp distinction between God and nature, revealing God as totally other than nature yet personally involved in it (Gen. 1-2:4). It reveals God as the elusive, transcendent one who will not be domesticated or brought under human control. It thereby recognizes the constant danger of idolatry, of identifying God with the forces of nature or, more subtly, turning God into a yes-man sanctioning the religious or cultural *status quo* (Ex. 20:4; Deut. 5:7-9).

The Old Testament, furthermore, reveals a unique view of human beings. We are finite, temporal creatures, dependent upon God in every moment for life and for all gifts and capacities (Gen. 1-2). We are not "rugged individuals," carrying the burden of self-establishment and self-fulfillment. Rather, God intends for us to live in a community, as a people living holy, obedient, and trusting lives under his lordship (Ex. 4:22; Deut. 8:5, 32:18; Isa. 1:2, 63:8, 16; Jer. 3:19; Hos. 11:1).

The Old Testament, in short, provides the basic framework for viewing all of life as lived under God. The New Testament largely assumes that framework and builds upon it. In providing that framework, the Old Testament thereby enables us to critique other worldviews as they compete with a biblical worldview.

Neglect or eclipse of the Old Testament, for this reason, makes us more vulnerable to misalliances with secular or naturalistic worldviews. It encourages what someone called "*Reader's Digest* religion"—the popular American folk religion that turns God into the pleasant "man upstairs" and equates God's will with the fulfillment of human wants and desires.[21]

Today Churches of Christ remain theologically ill-equipped, for with our "Old Testament Removed" we lack vital resources for recognizing and critiquing the secular worldviews that long have shaped the church and now threaten to dominate it. We must rediscover Old Testament theology and the essential resources it provides for constructing a biblical worldview. We must embrace the whole canon of Scripture and thereby become a more biblical people.

Attending to Biblical Literature

A third step toward a fresh engagement with Scripture involves serious attention to its diverse literary forms. As we saw in chapter two, the scientific, rationalistic approach to the Bible valued precise, factual, propositional language. It tended to reduce Scripture to one form: the logical, discursive, and merely factual. It largely overlooked another (complementary) route to truth—the way routed through story, poetry, parable, and metaphor. With Acts and the Pauline Epistles as our canon-within-a-canon this was somewhat easy to do. For it is the Old Testament and the Gospels, largely, which present us with what we might call a biblical literature of the imagination.

Recognizing different literary forms or genre in Scripture greatly affects one's interpretation. Consider an analogy from the world of sports. We enjoy a great variety of sports—track and field, gymnastics, swimming and diving, basketball, ice skating, skiing, golf, and baseball, for example. Each sport requires different standards of measurement or evaluation. Each set of standards must be specifically suited to the particular sport. Thus, judges do not evaluate a long jump with a stop watch or a high dive with a tape measure. They do not rate a pole vault on a point scale (as in diving). In each case proper criteria for evaluation must be drawn from the activity itself.

The same principle applies to the various types of biblical literature. Reading biblical poetry, parables, stories, letters, and hymns as one reads a constitution, a legal document, or a scientific treatise utterly distorts them. It is to ask questions that the texts were not designed to answer, to make demands they cannot supply. It is like evaluating a freestyle figure skating routine with a tape measure.

To extend our sports analogy further, notice something else: applying the standards correctly often demands extensive experience with the sport itself. Take a novice basketball referee. Obviously he must know the rule book. He must know, for instance, how it distinguishes a blocking foul from a charging foul. But no matter how well our novice referee knows what the rule book says about blocking fouls and charging fouls, he will become a competent referee only as he observes many drives to the basket and thus grows proficient in the skill of distinguishing one kind of foul from another. He will be a good referee, in other words, only when he has developed a trained eye and a "feel" for the game.

The same principle applies to interpreting literature. One interprets a poem best who loves poetry, reads its frequently, and perhaps fancies herself something of a poet. One interprets stories best who, time and again, has experienced the power of a good story and, in the process, gained the capacity to enter imaginatively into the storyworld. In general, one interprets literature best who has discovered, as Elie Wiesel put it, that "words can sometimes, in moments of grace, attain the quality of deeds."

My point is that in our interpretation of the Bible we must turn from a predominantly "scientific" model to literary/ historical ones. But here again we may find ourselves exploring a strange and unfamiliar world—a world that questions, revises, or even sets aside our modern, scientific penchant for nailing things down and closing them up. Stories, poems, parables, and hymns, to the contrary, open things up. They envision the new and the unexpected. They flirt with mystery and the "impossible." They perceive what those who only measure, manage, and analyze cannot perceive. A strange world indeed.

To help us enter that literary world somewhat, I turn now to six basic types (or genres) of biblical discourse. These six are not exhaustive and they overlap considerably. But they do show something of what a literary reading of Scripture involves.[22]

(1) *Narrative.* At the heart of the Bible, as any serious reader soon discovers, lies a basic story line. That story recounts the Lord's great deeds in the history of Israel and in the life of the earliest Christians. Along the way it branches out into many complex, sometimes gripping, sometimes tedious subplots. Furthermore, it incorporates instructional materials, songs, poems, prophetic oracles in poetic form, wisdom sayings, and letters. In times of crisis and renewal the key episodes of the story get retold and reinterpreted in surprising ways thus becoming in some sense an ever-new story.

The narrative genre dominates large sections of the Bible: the Pentateuch, the historical books, the Gospels, and Acts. The narratives fall into two basic types. Some narrate history—the history, for example, of Saul, David, and Israel's kings (in the books of Samuel and Kings), and of Jesus' ministry and the growth of the church (in sections of the Gospels and Acts). Other narratives make no claim to narrate history at all (as in Jesus' parables).

Consider the narratives in 1 and 2 Samuel and in Luke/ Acts, for example. These narratives present factual or historical truth to a considerable extent, but it is not simply factual. Rather, it is saving truth. It is truth explaining what God is doing in human history and which will stir the appropriate response in those who hear or read it. The stories show that God worked in the history of David to bless and deliver Israel, and that in the history of Jesus God worked to bless all the human race. They are not just presenting facts but rather trying to persuade us of their significance for our lives.

The non-historical narratives function in similar ways. With the parables of Jesus, for example, our primary questions should not be, "Did they happen?" or "What are the facts?" but rather, "What are these stories trying to do? How do they fit in the larger story of Jesus' ministry? And how do they shape life in the kingdom?"

Here we must grasp a most basic point: much of a story's power lies in the very fact that it is a story. Stories are dynamic and alive. They go somewhere. Things happen. Relationships form, grow, fail, and experience healing. God acts. Unlikely people get transformed.

Take David's story, for instance. We read it and feel the tenderness and innocence of the shepherd boy days. We tremble with him before Goliath and feel the rush of victory. We peer with him into the night, lusting for Bathsheba. We lie with him on his bed at three o'clock in the morning, heartsick and weary with remorse. We read Psalm 51, find cleansing, taste the severity and kindness of the Lord. David's story takes us somewhere. In our own lives, we all, in one way or another, may have been there before. But the story makes us see it more clearly, feel it more deeply, find mercy more necessary.

Reducing the story to something more logically precise, something more neatly packaged, violates it. It turns the dynamic into the static. It turns the growing process into fixed points, participation into memorization. It is like using a stop watch on a broad jump.

Or take the parables of Jesus. The scientific or rationalistic approach insists that in reading a parable one must extract "the point." The parable in this view becomes simply an illustration of some rather straightforward but abstract idea. The interpreter must simply extract that idea or principle.

Missing in this approach is the sense of parables as extended metaphors. "At its simplist," C. H. Dodd wrote, "the parable is a metaphor or simile drawn from nature or common life, arresting the hearer by its vividness or strangeness, and leaving the mind in sufficient doubt about its precise application to tease it into active thought." "Parables are tiny bits of coal squeezed into diamonds," Walter Wink says, "condensed metaphors that catch the ray of something ultimate and glint it at our lives. Parables are not illustrations; they do not support, elaborate, or simplify a more basic idea. They are not ideas at all, nor can they ever be reduced to theological statements. They are the jeweled portals of another world." They contain a "surplus of meaning that beckons us beyond ourselves to discover something new." They have "hooks all over them; they can grab each of us in a different way, according to our need."[23]

Viewing parables as extended metaphors, however, certainly does not mean that one can cut them loose from their original settings. The biblical parables, like all effective metaphors, are rooted in a particular time and place. The interpreter must always attempt to read them in context, which means attending both to their historical setting (first-century Palestine) and to their literary context (a particular Gospel account).[24]

But because they are metaphors, the parables do not so much provide new facts as they do new horizons. They do not simply convey new information; rather, they act upon the hearer in subtle but profound ways. The one who hears them goes away with new perspectives on life in the kingdom, with new wisdom, new challenges, new and richer emotions.

The parable of the Prodigal Son in Luke 15, for example, does not simply provide a good illustration of some point Jesus wished to make. For one thing the outcome remains unresolved. We wonder: "Will the prodigal remain a loyal son when the going gets tough? Will the older brother ever really accept him? And will the father's seemingly easy acceptance of the wayward son lead to further license?" The story provides no answers. It does not resolve our questions. Instead we are drawn into the story and forced to decide for ourselves. We are compelled to ask: "Where do I fit in the story? And what does that mean?"

Biblical narratives do not just present the "facts." We cannot simply reduce them in order to abstract their doctrinal content, for the stories themselves possess an inherent power. As Stanley Hauerwas put it, the biblical stories are "not secondary for our knowledge of God; there is no 'point' that can be separated from the story. The narratives through which we learn of God are the point. Stories are not substitute explanations we can some day hope to supplant with more straightforward accounts."[25] In this view doctrines are not so much the point of stories but rather the conceptual tools to help us tell the stories properly.

The biblical stories entice us to identify with the characters, to face their dilemmas, to see their strengths and weaknesses as perhaps a mirror of our own, to see God at work, and to experience with them both God's judgment and mercy. The biblical stories bring our small self-centered worlds into collision with the new, unexpected, and life-giving world where God reigns.

(2) *Law Code.* We find a second major genre of biblical literature in the law codes interspersed throughout the Old Testament narratives [such as the Decalogue (Ex. 20:1-17; Deut. 5:6-21), the Covenant Code (Ex. 20:22-23:33), the Holiness Code (Lev. 19-26), and the Deuteronomic Code (Deut. 12-26)].

We seriously misconstrue these materials if we simply think of them as "law" in our usual, modern sense of the word. For one thing, these codes are set within a narrative framework—the story of God's mighty acts of deliverance. In leading the Israelites out of Egyptian captivity, God redeemed them. Israel experienced the Lord's gracious and mighty salvation. Then at Sinai, following this deliverance, God offered his covenant to the people:

> You have seen what I did to the Egyptians, and how I bore you on eagles' wings and brought you to myself. Now therefore, if you will obey my voice and keep my covenant, you shall be my own possession among all

peoples; for all the earth is mine, and you shall be to me a kingdom of priests and a holy nation (Ex. 19:4-6a).

Loved, chosen, and redeemed by God, the people enter, at God's invitation, into covenant relationship with him. They pledge themselves to obedience and holiness. They say, "All that the Lord has spoken we will do" (19:8). They realize that their whole life and future depends on God's grace and promise.

Through his covenant, then, God invited his chosen people into a close, intimate relationship with him. They were no longer slaves but God's "firstborn son" whom he had graciously redeemed (Ex. 4:22). To aid this relationship God revealed the Ten Commandments and then other covenant obligations. Out of deep gratitude the people of Israel responded with obedience, seeking thereby to deepen the relationship, to live holy lives, and to bring glory to their deliverer.

Note clearly: the "good news" of God's love and deliverance preceded the giving of the law. Grace took priority over law. Salvation did not depend upon keeping the law perfectly—it was not a legal accomplishment at all. It was a gracious act of God. But salvation *did* bring responsibility. The experience of saving grace *did* bring with it the sacred obligations of covenant.[26]

The whole story of God's mighty acts—creation, the promises to the fathers, the election of Israel, the exodus, the covenant relationship, the giving of the law—this whole story became known as torah, meaning "teaching" or "instruction." Torah, encompassing both law and narrative, became the source for Israel's identity as the people of God.

We must remember however that torah was not "law" in our often narrow usage of the word. It was not simply divine commands and human obligations. It was not legalism. Rather it was the story of God's love and might, of divine graciousness and deliverance. It was a guide to holiness and a mandate for justice. It was a source of life. It was joy and wisdom, understanding and well-being.

The psalmist was speaking of torah in this sense when he wrote:

> The law of the Lord is perfect,
>   reviving the soul;

The testimony of the Lord is sure,
  making wise the simple;
The precepts of the Lord are right,
  rejoicing the heart;
The commandment of the Lord is pure,
  enlightening the eyes (Ps. 19:7-8).[27]

Reading the biblical law codes apart from their narrative setting would be like reading the baseball rule book without thrilling to the game itself.

(3) *Letter.* In the New Testament letters constitute one of the major literary genres. In this regard recent scholarship has shown that New Testament letters reflect the forms and literary conventions of letter writing in the Jewish and Greco-Roman worlds.

Paul's letters provide the chief example. Like most ancient letters, they include three basic parts: an opening formula, a main body, and a closing formula. The main bodies of the letters include several types of material common to ancient letters. They contain autobiographical statements (1 Thess. 1:2-3:13; Gal. 1:10-2:21) and discussions of travel plans (Rom. 1:8-15, 15:14-33; 1 Cor. 4:14-21, 16:1-11). They frequently include formulaic blessings reflecting the Jewish pattern of blessing (Rom. 1:25, 9:5; 2 Cor. 1:3-4, 11:31) and traditional doxologies ascribing glory to God (Phil. 4:20; Rom. 11:36; Gal. 1:5).

Further, Paul's letters occasionally incorporate early Christian hymns or hymn fragments (Rom. 11:33-36; Phil. 2:6-11; Col. 1:15-20) and early Christian confessions of faith (Rom. 10:9, 4:24-25, 8:34; 1 Cor. 15:3-5; 2 Cor. 5:15). And they commonly contain vice and virtue lists (Gal. 5:19-23; 2 Cor. 6:6-7; 1 Cor. 5:10-11) and codes of household ethics (Col. 3:18-4:1; Titus 2:1-10) which closely parallel those of Greco-Roman writings.[28]

But the most important literary feature of New Testament letters is this: they are *occasional documents.* That is, they were occasioned by specific circumstances and addressed to specific persons in the first century. They were not written, in the first instance, directly to you or me, to your congregation or mine. As inspired Scripture they first addressed the situation of the original audience. Today these letters instruct us in vital ways, to be sure; but in order for them to do that properly, we must first attend as best we can to the original circumstances and recipients.

To see the occasional nature of the New Testament letters more clearly, suppose for a moment that two of Paul's letters got sent to the wrong churches. Suppose, for example, that Paul wrote his passionate, sometimes angry Galatian letter and his sober First Thessalonian letter about the same time. Suppose further that, in sending them, an assistant mixed up the envelopes. The Galatian letter ends up in Thessalonica and the Thessalonian letter ends up in a Galatian church. Just suppose.

What would have been the result? Each church, no doubt, would have quickly recognized the mistake. Further, after reading the entire letter, each church would realize that it had learned something about a situation far removed from its own and about how Paul addressed that situation. But neither church could read the letter as a personal message from Paul. To apply the misdirected letters, each church would have to do considerable "translation." Each group would have to give considerable thought to how a message directed specifically to another group could be applied to itself.[29] Today we face just such a challenge when we read the Pauline letters.

The point simply is that good interpretation demands that we take the occasional nature of the New Testament letters seriously. As we do, these ancient letters—originally addressed to others—will still speak to us with divine power and insight.

(4) *Prophetic Oracle.* In the prophetic books of the Hebrew Bible we find another basic literary genre: the prophetic saying or oracle. Oracles are sayings in which a prophet proclaims a message received from the Lord. They usually begin with a phrase like "thus says the Lord" or "hear the word of the Lord," thus indicating that the prophet speaks not by his own authority but as the Lord has commissioned him (e.g., Amos 7:14-17; Jer. 9:1-3).

The authority of the prophet's oracles arose out of the prophet's call. The great prophets like Amos, Hosea, Isaiah, Jeremiah, and Ezekiel received an unexpected, awe-inspiring, often disruptive call to the prophetic vocation (Amos 7; Isa. 6;

Jer. 1; Ezek. 2-3). Amos for example exclaimed, "Yahweh kidnapped me from behind my flock" (7:15). Caught off guard, seized by God, the prophets received the divine commission.

They told the story of those experiences in "call narratives." Jeremiah's call provides a classic example (Jer. 1:4-10). First, God confronted him; he heard the powerful and active word of God. Second, God commissioned him. Third, Jeremiah objected; he protested his inadequacy for the divinely appointed task. Fourth, God reassured him, promising sustenance as Jeremiah speaks the divine word. And fifth, God gave Jeremiah a sign, thus convincing him that God would provide the message.

Out of such experiences the prophets received the divine word and proclaimed it under divine compulsion. We must see, however, that in the process of carrying out their commission they exercised a powerful literary artistry. They adapted conventional literary forms as vehicles for their messages. So we find oracles of judgment, oracles of repentance, oracles of future deliverance, woe oracles, and covenant lawsuits, for example. In addition we find doxologies or short hymns of praise (as in Amos 5:8-9), lengthy hymns (as in Isaiah 40-55), individual laments (as in Jeremiah's "confessions"), the dirge or funeral song (as in Ezek. 19:2-14), and other poetic forms.[30]

Throughout the various types of oracles we must not miss the fact that the prophets were poets of great skill and power. One scholar calls them "poets of divine presence." In their utterances, another says, they "put words to things until their teeth rattled." They employed rich images and powerful metaphors. Listen to Amos, for example:

> Hear this word, you cows of Bashan,
>   who are in the mountain of Samaria,
> who oppress the poor, who crush the needy,
>   who say say to their husbands, "Bring, that we
>   may drink!" (Amos 4:1)

Or to Hosea's vision of Israel's restoration:

> They shall go after the Lord,
>   he will roar like a lion;
> yea, he will roar,
>   and his sons shall come trembling from the west;

they shall come trembling like birds from Egypt,
  and like doves from the land of Assyria;
  and I will return them to their homes, says the Lord.
  (Hos. 11:10-11)

Or to Isaiah's poem, perhaps the greatest of them all:

Who has believed what we have heard?
  And to whom has the arm of the Lord been revealed?
For he grew up before him like a young plant,
  and like a root out of a dry ground;
he had no form or comeliness that we should look at him,
  and no beauty that we should desire him. . . .
But he was wounded for our transgressions,
  he was bruised for our iniquities;
upon him was the chastisement that made us whole,
  and with his stripes we are healed. (Isa. 53:1-5)

These prophet/poets "put words to both the wonder and the horror of the world," Frederick Buechner wrote, "and the words can be looked up in the dictionary or the biblical commentary and can be interpreted, passed on, understood, but because these words are poetry, are image and symbol as well as meaning, are sound and rhythm, maybe above all are passion, they set echoes going the way a choir in a great cathedral does, only it is we who become the cathedral and in us that the words echo."[31]

Reading the prophetic oracles as something other than poetry is like scoring a basketball game using something other than baskets.

(5) *Wisdom*. The wisdom writings (Job, Proverbs, Ecclesiastes, and several "wisdom" Psalms) comprise another major literary genre of Scripture. To understand this body of literature we must observe some of its basic features.

First, wisdom literature deals less with what God reveals (through prophetic word or mighty acts) than with what human beings can discover about the world. "Broadly speaking," R. B. Y. Scott comments, "the prophet speaks from the standpoint of revelation, the wise man from that of reason working from the data of experience and observation."[32]

Thus Proverbs for example argues against sex with prostitutes not so much on the ground that it violates a direct command of God—though it does—but on the basis that it results in nothing but trouble (Prov. 2:16-19). The wisdom writings ask questions like "What is useful? What is destructive and enslaving? What kind of behavior results in anguish?" It stresses what a discerning person can look around and see to be true about the way life usually works.

Failure to take this feature of proverbs into account leads to serious misinterpretation. Take a well-known proverb that has troubled many godly parents: "Train up a child in the way he should go; and when he is old he will not depart from it" (22:6). Here "train up a child" is not a commandment (as you might find in the torah) and "when he is old" is not a prophecy (as you might find in prophetic oracles). It is simply a proverb. It simply observes that adults usually reflect the training they received as children.

Second, wisdom literature rests on the presupposition that God has created an orderly world and that the perceptive observer can trace those regularities. We must not view Old Testament wisdom simply as the best of human insight or the storehouse of accumulated human wisdom. Rather, it is the product of attentive observation and the teasing out of divine truth embedded within the created order. Thus in the very process of dealing with the workings of creation, it deals with the God who created it.

Third, wisdom literature is characterized by a stress on "common sense." Fools are distinguished from the wise precisely in that fools lack common sense and thus cannot see the world for what it so clearly is. This common sense also means *shared* sense in that it stands in a *tradition* of observing and commenting on the world. The outlook of the wise man, in other words, is shaped by a heritage of wisdom, not simply his own observations (Prov. 6:20, 23).

Fourth, wisdom literature is marked by a recognition of the limits of wisdom. An important theme in Proverbs and especially Ecclesiastes and Job is that divine wisdom always limits human wisdom, that human plans and insights always come up short before the boundless and inscrutable purposes of God (cf. Job. 28:12-13, 23-24; Eccles. 8:16-17). Such recognition of the limits of wisdom leads ultimately to the claim that true wisdom is the gift of God. Though making a large place for human abilities, discoveries, and "common sense," biblical wisdom finally acknowledges that "it is the Lord who gives wisdom: from his mouth come knowledge and understanding" (Prov. 2:6; cf. Prov. 1:7, Job 28:28).[33]

The genre of wisdom writing occupies a modest place in the canon of Scripture. It calls us to use our minds but never to deify them, to acknowledge the appropriateness of human reason but with humble deference to the hidden purposes of God. Reading the wisdom materials as if they were torah, prophetic oracle, or apostolic letter distorts them. It would be like using a golf score card on a soccer game.

(6) *Psalm and Hymn.* Another major literary genre in Scripture is the psalm. Though found primarily in the book of Psalms, it also appears in various forms in the torah (Ex. 15:1-18), the historical books (2 Sam. 23:2-7), the prophetic books (Isa. 40-55), the wisdom writings (Job 28), and the New Testament letters (Phil. 2:5-11).

The biblical psalms, for the most part, are musical poems addressed to God. They are not, in the first instance, direct words *from* God as we find in some parts of Scripture, but rather words spoken *to* or *about* God. And yet, because they are part of the biblical canon, these words originally addressed to God also address us today as God-approved words.

If Israel's prophets were "poets of divine presence," as we have seen, then Israel's early psalmists were "poets of the interior quest."[34] Notice two things about their work. First, their songs emerged out of personal experience and reflect an intense inwardness. Out of David's experience of deliverance from enemies (2 Sam. 22), for example, comes the great psalm of thanksgiving (Ps. 18):

> He reached from on high, he took me,
>   he drew me out of many waters.
> He delivered me from my strong enemy,
>   and from those who hated me. . .
> He brought me forth into a broad place (vss. 16-17, 19).

Or out of the experience of searing guilt comes a psalm of confession and forgiveness (Ps. 51). The Psalms emerged not only out of the intense experience of divine presence but often out of the anguished experience of divine absence (Ps. 22).

Second, Israel's psalmists wrote their songs in response to God—to God's creative marvels, to God's mighty acts of deliverance, to God's graciousness, to the awesomeness of divine presence, and often to God's troubling silence or inexplicable absence.

We can divide Israel's psalms into three major forms: psalms of praise, psalms of lament and supplication, and psalms of thanksgiving.

The laments make up one of the largest groups (about a third of the Psalter).[35] They typically follow a general pattern consisting of five parts. Consider Psalm 10, for example. First, the psalmist begins with a *cry to God*:

> Why dost thou stand afar off, O Lord?
> Why dost thou hide thyself in times of trouble?

Second, he offers his *lament* or complaint (vss. 2-11). Employing vivid images and hyperbole, the psalmist paints a graphic portrait of the wicked people in his society who oppress the helpless:

> His eyes stealthily watch for the hapless,
>   he lurks in secret like a lion in his covert;
> he lurks that he may seize the poor,
>   he seizes the poor when he draws him into his net
>   (vs. 8-9).

Third, the psalmist makes a *plea for divine deliverance* (vss. 12, 15):

> Arise, O Lord; O God, lift up thy hand;
>   forget not the afflicted. . .
> Break thou the arm of the wicked and evildoer;
>   seek out his wickedness till thou find none.

Fourth, the psalmist expresses his *confidence in God* (vss. 13-14, 16-18):

> O Lord, thou wilt hear the desire of the meek;
>   thou wilt strengthen their heart,

thou wilt incline thine ear
to do justice to the fatherless and the oppressed,
so that man who is of the earth may strike terror no
more.

Fifth, the psalmist expresses *praise or thanksgiving to God:*
The Lord is king for ever and ever;
the nations shall perish from his land (vs. 16).

The psalms of praise and thanksgiving also follow certain patterns. The point is that we must read the Psalms as musical poems arising out of the psalmists' experience and shaped by the worship life of Israel. Reading them as something else is like scoring a track meet as if it were a baseball game.

In this section I have looked at six of Scripture's most important literary forms. These six are not exhaustive but only illustrative. By focusing on them I am simply urging that we move from a predominantly "scientific" model (in which Scripture is primarily a collection of doctrinal "facts") to a literary/historical model (in which we focus on historical setting and on literary form and function). Given our familiar, traditional way of reading the Bible, however, such a move may well mean breaking with tradition and entering a strange and unfamiliar world.

Following the Plot

A fourth step toward a fresh engagement with Scripture involves renewed attention to following its plot, that is, to locating Scripture's central story and central themes.

Our traditional "scientific" way of reading Scripture, as we have seen, tended to level Scripture into a body of doctrinal facts. These facts, when inductively assembled into their proper order, all carried about the same weight. As a result, distinctions between majors and minors, between the main plot and various subplots, were lost. Scripture lost its narrative texture, and thus we lost the ability to follow the movement of the text with its twists and turns, high points, and central themes.

Throughout the history of our movement, as a result, we have struggled endlessly with the problem of what is essential and what is not essential. This struggle began with Campbell himself. He wrote in 1826 that "We are always to distinguish what is merely circumstantial in any institution from the institution itself." He then proposed two rules by which one could do this. First, a practice employed by only one church, rather than universally in the church as a whole, was not essential or binding. Second, he stated that "all instituted acts of religion are characterized by the definite article, as *the* Lord's table, *the* Lord's day, &c."[36]

But Campbell did not follow his principles consistently over the years. In 1826 a German Baptist wrote to Campbell asking why he refused to extend the concept of restoration to clear New Testament practices like footwashing, the holy kiss, and others. Regarding the holy kiss, for example, he argued (counter to his earlier principles) that, since it was commanded five times in the Epistles, it was not an essential ordinance. Essential practices, he now said, were assumed by the New Testament writers, not commanded.[37]

The problem of essentials has plagued Churches of Christ ever since, leading frequently to rancor and fragmentation. Behind this problem lies the Baconian inductive method where one pulls down the concordance, gathers the biblical "facts," then constructs a doctrinal platform with each plank of virtually equal weight. With this way of reading the Bible, we have simply not been able to follow the biblical plot and thus to let what is theologically central in Scripture function centrally for us.

A literary/historical model, rather than our traditional "scientific" model, will serve the text better. It will help us better distinguish Scripture's main plot from the various subplots, what is primary from what is secondary.

Turning to the Old Testament, for example, we can find Israel's most fundamental credo (or root story) in several key texts (Ex. 15:1-18; Deut. 26:5-9; 6:20-24; Josh. 24:1-13; Neh. 9; Ps. 136).[38]

From these texts and others we can summarize Israel's basic story (or "primal narrative") as follows:

(1) Yahweh made a promise to the fathers in the midst of great precariousness.

(2) With a great display of divine power, Yahweh delivered Israel out of slavery.

(3) God led Israel in the wilderness, entered into covenant relationship with the people, and sustained them in their arduous pilgrimage.

(4) God fulfilled his promise by bringing Israel into a good land, and the people delighted in all the Lord's goodness.

(5) But time and again Israel rebelled against God and spurned his statutes; God thus delivered them to their enemies; but when they cried out to him, he graciously delivered them.

(6) Finally, after many prophetic warnings, Israel and Judah were carried off into exile. Eventually God returned a faithful remnant to their homeland, where they eagerly looked for God's future vindication and exaltation.

In the New Testament, likewise, we find the basic story (or "primal narrative") of the earliest Christian community (1 Cor. 1:23; 15:3-8; sermons in Acts).[39] It can be summarized as follows:

(1) The new age or epoch promised in Israel's Scriptures has dawned in the coming of Christ.

(2) Jesus died to deliver us out of the present evil age, was buried, and rose from the dead on the third day according to the Scriptures.

(3) Because of his resurrection, God exalted Jesus to his right hand and crowned him Lord of the living and the dead.

(4) The Holy Spirit's presence in the church indicates that Jesus lives and abides with those who believe in him.

(5) Jesus will come again to consummate his Kingdom, serving as judge and savior of all people.

(6) Upon hearing this message, people are urged to repent and be baptized, thus receiving God's offer of forgiveness and of the gift of the Holy Spirit.

This story forms the theological center of the New Testament. By focusing on the theological centers of Scripture we can better allow what is central in God's story to stand at the center of our story.

Conclusion

In this chapter I have offered four suggestions for a fresh engagement with Scripture. I have urged that we (1) recognize the remoteness of the biblical text and make a commitment to historical interpretation; (2) enlarge our functional canon by making the Old Testament and the Gospels more central in our theology; (3) read Scripture as a collection of diverse literature rather than simply as a collection of "facts"; and (4) attempt to follow the central story, thereby distinguishing what is primary from what is secondary.

We should not fear a new reading of Scripture today. If our early forebears have taught us anything, it should be a readiness to test our traditions and read the Bible afresh, for that has been the highest ideal of this restoration movement.

But as we attempt to do that today, we must resist a certain temptation. We must resist the temptation to think that, while our spiritual forebears fell short in their approach to Scripture, we—with some great burst of illumination—can finally unlock the magic door into theological perfection. We must not imagine for a moment that we have found the one interpretive method that will put every piece into place once and for all. Such presumption we must put behind us. For we do not master Scripture the way many modern scientists presume to master nature. Thinking that we can, in fact, easily becomes a kind of idolatry, as we will see in the next chapter.

Missing in such a presumption is a most basic confession—our creatureliness. This fundamental confession contains no license for abandoning our movement's high ideals or for relaxing our efforts to read Scripture correctly. Neither does it sanction disregard for reasonableness and coherence in the pursuit of truth. But it does demand that we confess our finitude and frailty as a fundamental theological maxim.

Such a confession, far from discouraging hard Bible study and serious theological reflection, will serve rather to enhance it. For making that confession will lift from our shoulders the unbearable burden of self-establishment before God. It will constantly drive us to the cross and thereby keep the good news always resounding in our ears. In the process, it will free us to ask new questions and to live—as we sometimes must—with provisional answers.

The confession of our creatureliness also helps us recognize that biblical interpretation is a corporate enterprise, that no one person possesses a wide enough range of spiritual and intellectual gifts to do the task alone. We need the gifts of many people who have submitted their lives to Christ. We need scholars and prophets, pastors and evangelists, women and men, old Christians and new Christians, cautious guardians and adventurous explorers. For we are not meant to be solitary readers of the Bible, "rugged individuals" left to our own devices. Rather, we are members of a body, drawing life from the head and working with one another in the fellowship of the Spirit. In that body we continually discover riches as, together, we explore the strange world of the Bible.

Notes

Epigraphs: Augustine, *Homilies on the Gospel of John,* 50. 6.; Walter Brueggemann, *Hopeful Imagination: Prophetic Voices in Exile* (Philadelphia: Fortress, 1987), p. 24.

[1]These examples come from Gailyn Van Rheenen, long-time missionary among the Kipsigis people.

[2]Fred Craddock, *As One Without Authority* (Nashville, Tenn.: Abingdon, 1981), p. 117.

[3]Alexander Campbell, *The Christian System, in Reference to the Union of Christians, and a Restoration of Primitive Christianity, as Plead in the Current Reformation,* 2nd ed. (Bethany, W.V., 1839; reprint ed., Nashville, Tenn.: Gospel Advocate, 1970), pp. 107-52.

[4]On Campbell's use of Locke's social compact theory and some of the problems it brought, see William D. Howden, "The Kingdom of God in Alexander Campbell's Hermeneutics," *Restoration Quarterly* 32 (Second Quarter 1990). For an indepth treatment of this metaphor in its Jewish setting, see G. R. Beasley-Murray, *Jesus and the Kingdom of God* (Grand Rapids, Mich.: Eerdmans, 1986).

[5]Edgar Krentz, *The Historical-Critical Method* (Philadelphia, Pa.: Fortress, 1975), pp. 64-65.

[6]Krister Stendahl, *Meanings: The Bible as Document and as Guide* (Philadelphia, Pa.: Fortress, 1984), p. 2.

[7]Lewis Thomas, *Late Night Thoughts on Listening to Mahler's Ninth Symphony* (New York: Bantam, 1984), p. 159. Acknowledging that scientists will need much help from others in answering all these questions, Thomas reflects a growing humility on the part of some scientists: "We have a wilderness of mystery to make our way through in the centuries ahead, and we will need science for this but not science alone. Science will, in its own time, produce the data and some of the meaning in the data, but never the full meaning. For getting a full grasp, we shall need . . . all sorts of brains outside the fields of science, most of all the brains of poets, but also those of artists, musicians, philosophers, historians, writers in general" (p. 150).

[8]I have adapted these models from Walter Wink, *Transforming Bible Study* (Nashville, Tenn.: Abingdon, 1981), pp. 85-87, and "The Education of the Apostles: Mark's View of Human Transformation," *Religious Education* 83 (Spring 1988):289-90.

[9]Andrew Louth, *Discerning the Mystery: An Essay on the Nature of Theology* (Oxford, Eng.: Oxford University, 1985), p. 145.

[10]Jesse L. Sewell, "Is the Bible a Mystery?" in David Lipscomb, *Life and Sermons of Jesse L. Sewell* (Nashville, Tenn.: Gospel Advocate, 1891), p. 133.

[11]Edwyn C. Hoskyns, *Cambridge Sermons* (London, Eng.: S.P.C.K., 1938), p. 70.

[12]Alexander Campbell, *Familiar Lectures on the Pentateuch*, ed. W. T. Moore (St. Louis, Mo.: Christian Publishing, 1867), pp. 266-304; *Christian Baptist* 1 (November 3, 1823):72. See Everett Ferguson, "Alexander Campbell's 'Sermon on the Law': A Historical and Theological Examination," *Restoration Quarterly* 29 (Second Quarter 1987):71-85.

[13]"A. Campbell's Reply to Ro. B. Semple," *Millennial Harbinger* 2 (January 3, 1831):15. Here Campbell refers to his "Sermon on the Law" as "my most juvenile essay."

[14]Eugene Boring, "The Formation of a Tradition: Alexander Campbell and the New Testament," *Disciples Theological Digest* 2 (1987):17-18. See also James Thompson, "New Testament Studies and the Restoration Movement," *Restoration Quarterly* 25 (1982):227.

[15]Alexander Campbell, *Christian System*, p. 133. Campbell can sometimes use the phrase "Acts and Epistles of the Apostles" as the functional equivalent of "New Testament" (e.g., p. 59).

[16]On the origin and role of the Gospels in the early church, see Keith Nickle, *The Synoptic Gospels: An Introduction* (Atlanta, Ga.: John Knox, 1982), and Luke T. Johnson, "Jesus in the Memory of the Church," in *The Writings of the New Testament: An Interpretation* (Philadelphia, Pa.: Fortress, 1986), pp. 114-40.

[17]Surveying nineteenth-century periodicals of the Stone/Campbell movement, Tony Ash concluded that "there was some concern with details of the Old Testament for their own sake; some use of the Old Testament to illustrate or explain New Testament references; and some citation of passages in the Old Testament believed to predict the coming of Christ and the Christian age. But other than that, the Old Testament was generally ignored. . . ." "Old Testament Studies in the Restoration Movement," *Restoration Quarterly* 9 (1966):216.

[18]The question of the relation between letter and spirit, Israel and church, Hebrew Bible and Greek Testament has been a formidable one for Christians from the earliest times. As David Steinmetz observes, "The Church regarded itself as both continuous and discontinuous with ancient Israel. Because it claimed to be continuous, it felt an unavoidable obligation to interpret the Torah, the prophets, and the writings. But it was precisely this claim of continuity, absolutely essential to Christian identity, that created fresh hermeneutical problems for the Church." "The Superiority of Pre-Critical Exegesis," *Theology Today* 37 (April 1980):29. For a good overview of how the early Christians approached the Hebrew Scriptures, see James L. Kugel and Rowan A. Greer, *Early Biblical Interpretation* (Philadelphia, Pa.: Westminster, 1986), pp. 113-51; for later historical developments see Richard N. Longenecker, "Three Ways of Understanding Relations between the Testaments: Historically and Today," in *Tradition and Interpretation in the New Testament*, ed. Gerald F. Hawthorne, with Otto Betz (Grand Rapids, Mich.: Eerdmans, 1987), pp. 22-32.

[19]Lee Martin McDonald, *The Formation of the Christian Biblical Canon* (Nashville, Tenn.: Abingdon, 1988), pp. 69-98, 120-45, and Harry Y. Gamble, *The New Testament Canon: Its Making and Meaning* (Philadelphia, Pa.: Fortress, 1985), pp. 23-56. An awareness of the gradual and somewhat fluid development of the New Testament canon throughout the first century clearly forces a rethinking of our traditional understanding of a New Testament pattern or blueprint (arrived at through scientific induction).

[20]See John Bright, *The Authority of the Old Testament* (London, Eng.: SCM, 1967), pp. 140-160, and Paul J. and Elizabeth Achtemeier, *The Old Testament Roots of Our Faith* (Philadelphia, Pa.: Fortress, 1962).

[21]Elizabeth Achtemeier, *The Old Testament and the Proclamation of the Gospel* (Philadelphia, Pa.: Westminster, 1973), pp. 37-44.

[22]These correspond somewhat to those outlined by Paul Ricoeur, "Toward a Hermeneutic of the Idea of Revelation," in *Essays on Biblical Interpretation*, ed. Lewis S. Mudge (Philadelphia, Pa.: Fortress, 1980), pp. 73-95.

[23]C. H. Dodd, *The Parables of the Kingdom* (London, Eng.: Nisbet & Co., 1956), p. 16; Walter Wink, *Transforming Bible Study*, pp. 159-61.

[24]See Robert Stein, *An Introduction to the Parables of Jesus* (Philadelphia, Pa.: Westminster, 1981), pp. 53-81, and John R. Donahue, *The Gospel in Parable: Metaphor, Narrative, and Theology in the Synoptic Gospels* (Philadelphia, Pa.: Fortress, 1988), pp. 1-27.

[25]Stanley Hauerwas, *The Peaceable Kingdom: A Primer in Christian Ethics* (Notre Dame, Ind.: University of Notre Dame, 1983), p. 26.

[26]On the priority of grace over law in the Torah, see George Braulik, "Law as Gospel: Justification and Pardon According to the Deuteronomic Torah," *Interpretation* 38 (January 1984):5-14.

[27]On Old Testament law, see Walter J. Harrelson, "Law in the Old Testament," *Interpreter's Dictionary of the Bible* (Nashville, Tenn.: Abingdon, 1962), 3:77-89; Achtemeier, *Old Testament Roots of Our Faith*, pp. 60-78; and Joseph Blenkinsopp, *Wisdom and Law in the Old Testament: The Ordering of Life in Israel and Early Judaism* (Oxford, Eng.: Oxford University, 1983), pp. 74-101.

[28]See David E. Aune, *The New Testament in Its Literary Environment* (Philadelphia, Pa.: Westminster, 1987), pp. 158-225, and Nils Dahl, "Letter," *Interpreter's Dictionary, Supplement*, pp. 538-41.

[29]This illustration was suggested by Willi Marxsen, *The New Testament as the Church's Book* (Philadelphia, Pa.: Fortress, 1972), p. 52.

[30]See for example Claus Westermann, *Basic Forms of Prophetic Speech*, trans. H. C. White (Philadelphia, Pa.: Westminster, 1967).

[31]Frederick Buechner, *Telling the Truth: The Gospel as Tragedy, Comedy, and Fairy Tale* (New York: Harper & Row, 1978), p. 21. Commenting on the dominance of poetry in prophetic speech, Robert Alter wrote: "Since poetry is our best human model of intricately rich communication, not only solemn, weighty, and forceful but also densely woven with complex internal connections, meaning, and implications, it makes sense that divine

speech should be represented by poetry." *The Art of Biblical Poetry* (New York: Basic Books, 1985), p. 141.

[32]R. B. Y. Scott, *The Way of Wisdom in the Old Testament* (New York: Macmillan, 1971), p. 113.

[33]On Israelite wisdom, see James L. Crenshaw, *Old Testament Wisdom: An Introduction* (Atlanta, Ga.: John Knox, 1981).

[34]Samuel Terrien, *The Elusive Presence: The Heart of Biblical Theology* (New York: Harper & Row, 1978), pp. 227, 279.

[35]On biblical psalmody, see Claus Westermann, *Praise and Lament in the Psalms* (Atlanta, Ga.: John Knox, 1981). On the laments, see also Walter Brueggemann, "From Hurt to Joy, from Death to Life," *Interpretation* 28 (1974):3-19.

[36]Alexander Campbell, "A Restoration of the Ancient Order of Things, No. VII," *Christian Baptist* 3 (September 5, 1825):30-31.

[37]Campbell, "Restoration of the Ancient Order, No. XI," *Christian Baptist* 3 (March 6, 1826):162-65. See also Thomas H. Olbricht, "Biblical Theology and the Restoration Movement," *Mission Journal* (1980): 4-9.

[38]Gerhard Von Rad, *Old Testament Theology*, trans. D. M. G. Stalker (New York: Harper & Row, 1960-1965), 1:121-28.

[39]C. H. Dodd, *The Apostolic Preaching and Its Development*, 2nd ed. (New York: Harper & Brothers, 1944), pp. 7-35.

4

The Living God and the Contest with Idols

The temptation to idolatry . . . is the greater the more man is surrounded by the works of his own hands.

—*H. Richard Niebuhr (1935)*

We can make a long list, from the Bible, of objects in which people from time to time reposed their hopes, only to find them all proved false. . . . God is continually weaning us from our false hopes, in order to lead us instead to the one Hope, which is—Himself.

—*C. F. D. Moule (1963)*

As we saw in chapter two, the secularizing forces unleashed in the Age of Reason changed the way people, including Christians, thought about God. The cosmos was mechanized and God became more distant and impersonal. God became more predictable, less mysterious, and eventually, for many people at least, less necessary.

As the sense of God's immediate and personal presence receded, Christians felt more and more compelled to prove God's reality, to make belief in God a matter of argument, evidence, and proof. Such attempts grew more intense as secularization progressed. Such attempts, in fact, partook of the secular assumptions that were becoming predominant in the

Age of Enlightenment, particularly the assumption that human reason was the ultimate authority and that everything—even God—must be subject to it. God, in the process, became something other than the God of Abraham, Isaac, and Jacob. Yahweh became a tame, manageable, and fathomable God for a secular, scientific age.

Secularization, whatever else it may involve, basically involves the displacement of the living God in human life and culture. To speak, then, of the secularization of the church or of the Christian faith is to speak of the displacement, distortion, and domestication of the God revealed in Scripture. In biblical terms it is to speak of idolatry. It is to speak of imagining, constructing, and reverencing gods that are in reality less than God.

Desecularization of the church, therefore, cannot proceed without raising, at the most fundamental level, the question of God. We must ask: How is idolatry possible today? Do we not often create God in our image? and, How does human sinfulness distort our perception of God? Then we must ask: Who is the God revealed in Scripture? What is this God like? How does God relate to his world and his creatures? And what kind of community does God call into being?

We may be tempted to focus our attention elsewhere. For after all, we believe in God. We honor and reverence God. We know who God is. So we easily assume that the true challenge lies elsewhere. It lies in materialism, or in sectarianism, or in leaders without vision, or in lack of church discipline, or in lack of unity, or in getting ourselves properly organized.

Our tradition among Churches of Christ makes it easy for us to think this way. For we have not focused on the biblical doctrine of God. We have tried to prove God's existence to some unbelievers, to be sure, and readily affirmed the so-called "classical attributes." But by and large we have not spent our energies engaging this most central of all biblical themes. Our controversies have not centered here, even though in Scripture the living God appears perpetually controversial. We most often simply assumed that we all understood the God Scripture reveals, and then turned to disputed doctrinal issues, most often regarding the form and structure of the church or human responsibility in salvation.

At least three factors in our history contributed to this neglect of the biblical doctrine of God. First, the Campbells and others among our early leaders, as heirs of the Puritans, focused restoration on the ordinances and structures of the church. Campbell himself underscored this emphasis. "The distinguishing characteristic [of the current reformation]," he wrote, "is, A RESTORATION OF THE ORDINANCES OF THE NEW INSTITUTION TO THEIR PLACE AND POWER" (Campbell's emphasis).[1]

Second, our early leaders, as heirs of the Enlightenment, possessed an Enlightened confidence in human ability to devise and implement a rational plan for unity. This confidence heightened the focus on churchly form and structure: emphasis fell on the exact reconstruction of the first apostolic community, then upon restoring and defending that pattern.[2]

Third, serious neglect of the Old Testament (as we saw in chapter three) played a key role, for it is there that we find much of what Scripture reveals about God's acts and character.

So we must grapple again with God. If secularization means a loss of transcendence, a reduction of God's majesty and mystery, then we must focus again on the living God as revealed in Scripture.

The Contest with Idols

The problem of idolatry provides perhaps the best place to start. For in Scripture we find that the contest with idols looms large throughout the history of God's people.

Consider first the Bible's strong and often repeated prohibitions against idolatry. The opening of the Decalogue states it most decisively: "You shall have no other gods before me. You shall not make for yourself a graven image, or any likeness of anything that is in heaven above, or that is in the earth beneath ... you shall not bow down to them or serve them; for I the Lord your God am a jealous God" (Ex. 20:3-5. Cf. 34:17; Lev. 19:4; and Deut. 5:7-9).

Moses relates this prohibition to Israel's experience with God at Sinai. "Since you saw no form on the day that the Lord spoke to you at Horeb out of the midst of the fire," Moses admonished, "beware lest you act corruptly by making a graven image for yourselves, in the form of any figure." They must not deify and worship any temporal thing, for the Lord alone is the creator and redeemer. It was the Lord, Moses told Israel, who "brought you forth out of the iron furnace, out of Egypt, to be a people of his own possession." The Lord offered them his covenant and they embraced it, pledging themselves to worship him alone. Forgetting the covenant and turning to idols would bring tragic results, Moses warned, for "the Lord your God is a devouring fire, a jealous God." He then concluded: "know therefore this day, and lay it to your hearts, that the Lord is God in heaven above and on the earth beneath; there is no other" (Deut. 4:15-16, 20, 23-24, 39).

But time and again Israel forgot the covenant with the Lord. Even while still camped at Sinai they forgot. At the people's insistence Aaron fashioned a golden calf, and when the Lord saw it he said to Moses: "Go down; for your people ... have turned aside quickly out of the way which I commanded them; they have made for themselves a molten calf, and have worshiped it and sacrificed to it, and said, 'These are your gods, O Israel, who brought you up out of the land of Egypt!'" (Ex. 32:7-8).

So begins the long saga of Israel's on-again-off-again love affair with other gods. The history of the judges, for example, is to a considerable degree a history of the contest with idols. One after another the stories begin with the often-repeated report: "they forsook the Lord, the God of their fathers, who had brought them out of the land of Egypt; they went after other gods, from among the gods of the peoples who were round about them; ...and they provoked the Lord to anger. They forsook the Lord, and served the Ba'als and Ash'taroth" (Jdgs. 2:12-13; cf. 2:17, 19; 3:7; 8:33; 10:6; 18:30-31). The yoke of oppression and slavery followed, then with the passing of time a cry of repentance, then a deliverer sent from the Lord.

With the rise of Israel's monarchy idolatry gained new impetus and power, for the kings themselves often led the way in promoting it. Solomon "turned away his heart after other gods"; he "worshiped Ashtoreth the goddess of the Sidonians,

Chemosh the god of Moab, and Milcom the god of the Ammon-
ites" (I Kgs. 11:4, 33). His successors in the divided kingdom followed suit. Jeroboam, king over the ten tribes in the north, set
up golden calves at Bethel and at Dan, then announced: "You
have gone up to Jerusalem long enough. Behold your gods, O
Israel, who brought you up out of the land of Egypt" (I Kgs.
12:28). And Rehoboam, king over Judah in the south, permitted
the people to build themselves "high places, and pillars, and
Asherim on every high hill and under every green tree" (I Kgs.
14:21-24).

  And so the story went from the time of Moses to the time
of the Exile in the early sixth century. The lure of idols remained
powerful and constant. For this reason the prophetic preaching
throughout this period gained much of its power from the stark
and uncompromising choice it presented between the Lord and
"other gods."[3] Elijah's ringing words as he began the great
contest with the prophets of Ba'al on Mt. Carmel exemplify the
prophetic challenge: "How long will you go limping with two
different opinions? If the Lord is God, follow him; but if Ba'al,
then follow him" (1 Kgs. 18:21).

  Most of the later prophets follow Elijah in setting forth
this clear and fateful choice between the living God and idols.
In the process they offer stinging rebukes. Hosea, for example,
utters this oracle from the Lord:

> They made kings, but not through me.
>   They set up princes, but without my knowledge.
> With their silver and gold they made idols
>   for their own destruction.
> I have spurned your calf, O Samaria.
>   My anger burns against them.
> How long will it be
>   till they are pure in Israel?
> A workman made it;
>   it is not God.
> The calf of Samaria
>   shall be broken to pieces (Hos. 8:4-6).

Despite such rebukes, however, the lure of idols remained
strong throughout much of Israel's history. The struggle never
seemed to let up.

I have often wondered why. Why was the worship of idols so appealing? Why did idols so mesmerize and attract Israel generation after generation? What was the allure? Modern and sophisticated people that we are, we find such questions hard to answer, I suspect. We think: did they not know that those crude, handmade images of wood or metal were not really divine? Could they not see that their golden calves were really nothing more than a product of the craftsman's art? What fools they were to devote themselves to such mundane things! What primitives!

In this reaction we can identify easily with the prophetic ridicule of idolatry. Isaiah, for example, points to the carpenter who cuts down a tree: "Half of it he burns in the fire; over the half he eats flesh, he roasts meat and is satisfied; also he warms himself and says, 'Aha, I am warm, I have seen the fire!' And the rest of it he makes into a god, his idol; and falls down to it and worships it; he prays to it and says, 'Deliver me, for thou art my god!'" (Isa. 44:16-17. Cf. 41:21-24, 28-29; 46:7). Jeremiah also puts it vividly:

> Their idols are like scarecrows in a cucumber field,
>   and they cannot speak;
> they have to be carried,
>   for they cannot walk (Jer. 10:5).

We get the point: it all seems so downright silly.

And in one way, of course, it is silly. But we must not dismiss it all so easily, as if those simple, gullible people could succumb to such silliness but that we sophisticates of course know better. For by making idolatry something remote and primitive, we overlook the possibility of idolatry today, in our own lives. We miss the dynamic of the idolatrous spirit.

First, consider this: in many cases, apparently, those who worshiped idols or images did not believe that the idol was actually the god itself. Rather, they believed that in some particularly powerful way the image represented the god or provided a sacred tie to the deity. Through the image the worshiper gained a more direct access to the divine power, thereby making the divine more subservient to his or her own interests and needs.

This points us to the heart of the idolatrous spirit. The Bible makes clear that idolatry, at its core, is a religious disguise for self-centeredness. Idols are projections of the human will. They represent attempts to make God less transcendent, less elusive, less sovereign and free, more at the beck and call of human interests. "The idols are the work of men's hands," Otto Baab wrote, "and the personal qualities they are alleged to possess are really ascribed to them by human beings by a magnificent process of self-deception. These idols are the glorified projections of the will of their human followers and supporters."[4]

We must see idolatry, in other words, as a function of self-love and self-deception. As a process, it contains two distinct movements: (1) treating something finite and created as absolute, and (2) in the process using it to serve the interests of the self.

This process works with great subtlety. We mask it with all sorts of evasions and rationalizations. For seldom do we simply announce openly our swelling pride or self-centeredness—or even admit it to ourselves. Rather, human self-centeredness most often assumes the form of idolatry, of allegiance to something beyond ourselves which we view as ultimately good (or as God) but which, in reality, we use to serve our own purposes. In this way, we subtly make God our servant, a projection of ourselves or of the interests of our social group.

An idol thus becomes any human-made alternative to God—anything that people devote their lives to, place their trust in, make sacrifices for, or in any way invest with ultimate significance. The prophet Hosea, for example, closely connects idolatry with devotion to material things like foreign alliances (5:13; 7:11), fortified cities (8:14), armies (10:13), and wealth (12:8). Anything at all that can break the bond of love and trust between God and God's people becomes an idol (3:1; 11:1-2).

We must see here a most basic biblical truth: *sin continually distorts our understanding of God, making us always susceptible to idolatry, to the worship of a god fashioned in our own image.* Paul puts it most strongly in Romans 1. God's invisible attributes, he insists, can be seen in the creation but sinners, refusing to honor or thank God, "exchanged the splendour of immortal God for an image shaped like mortal man, even for images like birds, beasts, and creeping things." Under the power of sin, people "bartered away the true God for a false one, and offered reverence and worship to created things instead of to the Creator" (Rom. 1:20-25, NEB).

Notice. For Paul the distorting power of sin leads not only to literal idolatry (the worship of physical images) but also to what we might call figurative idolatry (obsession with created things). He therefore can say pointedly that both coveteousness and gluttony are idolatry (Eph. 5:5; Col. 3:5; Phil. 3:19).[5]

Notice further. Paul here regards the tendency toward idolatry as so powerful and so central in human life that he attributes to it the fall of human society into all kinds of sin and self-delusion. We might say that for Paul humankind's alienation from all that is holy and good can be summed up in one word: idolatry.

With the biblical understanding of idolatry in view, we must admit that the idolatrous impulse appears even in our noblest efforts and our most prized convictions. H. Richard Niebuhr put it well:

> Men whose business it is to reason exalt reason to the position of judge and ruler of all things. . . . Those who have the vocation of maintaining order in society deify law—and partly themselves. The independent, democratic citizen has a little god inside himself in an authoritative conscience that is not under authority. As Christians we want to be the forgiver of sins, the lovers of men, new incarnations of Christ, saviors rather than saved; secure in our possession of the true religion, rather than dependent on a Lord who possesses us, chooses us, forgives us.[6]

Even the Bible itself or our own religious tradition can become idols. The Bible becomes an idol to the extent that we lose a sense of Scripture as mediating a divine reality which always transcends Scripture itself. It becomes an idol when our faith becomes focused on Scripture rather than in the God Scripture reveals to us. Our religious tradition (as we saw in chapter one) can become an idol to the extent that we absolutize it or make it identical in every respect to the Kingdom of God.

Our Christian faith remains vulnerable at every moment to idolatrous impulses. The very things we prize most deeply and believe in most ardently can become idols. Charles L. Loos, who taught with Alexander Campbell at Bethany College, had this tendency in mind when he spoke of "party idolatry." We easily get to the point where we think that "our views, our faith, our conduct, as a party, must be justified...," Loos wrote. "No man must raise even a doubt, or suggest any improvement or progress. If any one among us does not so 'glory,' and burn perpetual incense to this party idolatry, let him be marked as false, and be denounced at once."[7]

Behind this "party idolatry" stands a kind of "doctrine-idolatry." One becomes a "doctrine-idolater," Loos said, when one substitues "the means and the statements of the object, for the final object itself to be reached by these means." The "doctrine-idolater" thus forgets that

> Doctrines do not save us; we are saved by Christ. Doctrines do not cleanse us from our sins; it is the efficacious blood of Christ. We are not converted to doctrines, but to God.... We are not baptized into [doctrines], but into Christ. We do not hope in them, trust in them, glory in them, but in Christ Jesus our Lord.

Doctrines, he emphasized, only light the way to Christ and the cross; "they are but the divine forces to bring you to him. Rest not with the doctrine; bow not before it. Never stand still till you have arrived at the feet of Jesus on the Cross."[8]

We must not suppose, however, that the idolatrous impulse works only at the individual level. For this impulse works powerfully in and through the traditions and cultural forces that always surround us. The social dynamics of idolatry become clear when we look, for example, at the interplay between Israelite society and religion during the reign of Solomon. Notice three closely linked developments in this period.[9]

First, Solomon promoted *an economics of affluence and privilege*. Under Solomon's leadership Israel experienced unprecedented abundance. Many people enjoyed a high standard of living, with the king himself apparently enjoying the highest of all. "Solomon's provision for one day," we learn, "was thirty cors of fine flour, and sixty cors of meal, ten fat oxen, and twenty pasture-fed cattle, a hundred sheep, besides harts, gazelles, roebucks, and fatted fowl" (1 Kgs. 4:22-23). But though the king and many of his subjects ate sumptuously and lived luxuriously, not everyone did. Increasingly the abundant resources were distributed not on the basis of need but of privileged position (note for example the outcome of his regime in 1 Kgs. 11-12).

Second, Solomon employed *a politics of oppression*. Most obvious is his use of forced labor. "King Solomon raised a levy of forced labor out of all Israel; and the levy numbered thirty thousand men. And he sent them to Lebanon, ten thousand a month in relays. . . . Solomon also had seventy thousand burden bearers and eighty thousand hewers of stone in the hill country" (1 Kgs. 5:13-15).

Third, Solomon shaped *a religion of God's domestication*. He needed a God who would sanction his economics of affluence and his politics of oppression, a God who fully supported the exercise of royal power and privilege. So Solomon, we might say, created a more congenial God. He established "a controlled, static religion in which God and his temple have become part of the royal landscape, in which the sovereignty of God is fully subordinated to the purpose of the king."[10] God's presence became increasingly confined to the Jerusalem Temple, the worship of God increasingly institutionalized and controlled. Religion became acculturated, a reflection of the *status quo*. God became domesticated or secularized, a servant of royal policy. In the process, Solomon, not surprisingly, "turned his heart away after other gods." I say not surprisingly because the domestication of God in the service of personal, economic, and social concerns is nothing other than idolatry.

Forming God in Our own Image

The contest with idols—waged so often among the people of God—continues today. It continues due to a most basic fact: we are creatures prone, at every moment, to fashion God in our own image. We may affirm steadfastly the great biblical truth that God formed human beings in the divine image, that we each are unique and precious persons capable of relationship with the Creator. But we must also affirm the corollary truth that, sometimes out of ignorance but most often out of sinful pride, we also form God in our image. We make God a projection of what we want God to be. We make God reflect our values. We make God the special guardian of our race or nation. We call on God to sanction our way of life.

Examples abound in the history of Christianity of the ways believers do this. It becomes especially clear when we compare insiders and outsiders in a particular culture. By "insiders" I mean those who wield power and who enjoy the good life, and by "outsiders" I mean those who possess little power and who often live in poverty and oppression.

Christianity in the pre-Civil War American South provides a striking example. Slave-holding southern evangelicals, through a long and tortuous process of self-justification, developed a view of God and the Bible fully supporting the institution of slavery in which they held such high stakes. As one prominent southern Baptist preacher put it in a letter of 1848, "We who own slaves honor God's law in the exercise of our authority." At every turn southern theologians and preachers appealed to God and the Bible in support of that conclusion. They never tired of citing God's curse of Ham (Gen. 9:20-27), Paul's admonitions to slaves and masters (Eph. 6:5-9; Col. 4:1), and other Scriptures that could be used to support slavery.

The conclusions were obvious: southern institutions, including slavery, were divine institutions. Southern values were God's values. The southern God who ordained the institution of slavery was the biblical God, while the god of northern abolitionists was not God at all but the pagan god of nature or reason. The God of elite, southern whites was an insider's God, for they had formed him in their own image.[11]

The slaves, on the other hand, held a very different view of God. Their God valued and sanctioned very different things. Introduced to the Christian faith by their masters or by slave preachers, they appropriated a different set of biblical texts. They sang or recited texts like Isaiah 61:1, "The Lord has anointed me to . . . proclaim liberty to the captives." Or Acts

10:34, "God is no respector of persons." Or Matthew 23:10, "Call no man master, neither be ye called master." They identified with the Israelites enslaved in Egypt and celebrated the Exodus. Bearing their own crosses, they identified with Christ's crucifixion and in their worship exulted in the resurrection. "Enslaved, they sang of freedom; defeated, they awaited victory; powerless, they exercised the power of the 'righteous remnant.'"

The God of the slaves was the great Liberator. Their God identified with the suffering and defeated and himself stood with them outside the circle of power and respectibility. He heard the cries of enslaved blacks. He lifted up the weak and lowly and cast down the mighty from their thrones. The slaves were the outsiders and, like the white insiders, also formed God in their own image to some degree. But one thing stands out clearly: we are dealing here with two quite different Gods.[12]

We must not conclude that this way of thinking about God occurs only among slaves and slaveholders or other sharply contrasting outsider/insider groups. It occurs, in more subtle ways, among all social groupings in a culture. For not only do we form God in our own personal image, we also form God in the image of the social grouping to which we belong. Economic and social interests, in other words, inevitably color our perception of God.

Take middle-class, white Americans, for example. If we fit in this category, we will tend to believe in a middle-class, anglo-saxon American God. That is, the God we believe in most likely will sanction values and policies that protect and maintain middle-class American values. God becomes to some degree a projection of the economic and social values we hold dear and thus serves as the legitimator and preserver of those values.

So the God of middle-class white Americans views America as Number One or perhaps as the elect nation chosen to lead the world in the paths of righteousness. God sanctions the American work ethic where prosperity and affluence become signs of divine favor and poverty becomes a sign of moral failure. God becomes an ardent capitalist, a supporter of the nuclear arms race, a proponent of the "American dream." This

God may even lend cautious support to the credo that happiness is measured by pleasure and secured by material accumulation.[13]

God, in short, begins to sound alot like a successful, patriotic, upwardly-mobile, church-going American.

God thus becomes—subtly, to be sure—a projection of human values and wishes. The sociologist Emile Durkheim provided a helpful understanding of this phenomenon. He argued that every religion takes shape as a complex projection of a particular culture or social group. That is, the religion of a tribe, social class, or culture embodies the ideals of the group. The religion then serves as a kind of glue holding the group together and legitimating its ideals.

In this way the God of a frontier people possesses frontier values. The God of an affluent people sanctions and sanctifies affluence. The God of a warring people makes war holy. God and the other key elements of a religion thus reflect, through a process of projection, many of the collective traits and values of a social group. By this means religion provides social cohesion and vitality.[14]

Other modern analysts of religion have said similar things about how human beings form God in their own image. Consider what are perhaps the three most famous and influential critics of religion in modern times.

First was Ludwig Feuerbach (1804-1872) who believed that God was nothing but a projection of human wants and needs. "God springs out of the feeling of a want," he wrote in 1841; "what man is in need of, whether this be a definite and therefore conscious, or an unconscious need—that is God." Stated in more positive terms, this means that "whatever man wishes to be, he makes his God." In this view religion results from the human feeling of dependence, and God is nothing more than a product of the human ego.[15]

Second was Karl Marx (1818-1881) who viewed God as a consolation serving vested economic interests. Influenced heavily by Feuerbach's projection theory, Marx simply extended it to the economic arena. Economics, he claimed, determined the dominant image of God in a society. Thus in a feudal system one expects to find a feudal God presiding over things. In a capitalistic system one expects to find a capitalistic

God in charge. In each case God becomes a projection serving the financial interests of those who wield power in the prevailing system. Religion thereby becomes the opium of the masses, consoling them with promises of pie-in-the-sky in the great by-and-by.[16]

Third was Sigmund Freud (1856-1939) who viewed God as an infantile illusion that one clings to out of psychological need. As children, Freud argued, we are helpless in many ways and so depend on our parents for many things. We get used to relying on superior beings for help, so much so that when we grow up and find that we are still helpless in face of things like disease, injustice, and death, we seek a heavenly parent to guide and protect us. God thus becomes a psychological crutch. Religion becomes wishful thinking rooted in some kind of neurosis or other psychological immaturity.[17]

These critics of religion were atheists. That seems clear enough. But even so, I suggest that we need to hear them today and take their arguments seriously. For they saw, more clearly than most, our persistent and subtle drive to create gods in our own image. Indeed, as Feuerbach contended, we easily make God a projection of our wants and desires. Indeed, as Marx contended, we often make God reflect the values of our culture and sanction our privileged ways of life. And indeed, as Freud contended, our views of God are influenced greatly—both negatively and positively—by our childhood experiences with adults.

Such arguments, to be sure, say nothing about the actual existence or nonexistence of the living God revealed in Scripture. They overturn, not the living God, but only our narrow and self-serving views of God. They help expose the false gods created by the human imagination to serve narrow human ends. We too must seek to deny those gods.

It is striking in this regard that in the first few centuries of the church pagans sometimes charged that the Christians were "atheists." Why? How could people possibly have levelled such an incredible charge? The answer is simple: Christians denied the gods of the Roman state. They refused to worship the various gods that served the interests of the culture. They uttered a mighty "No!" to the gods that were projections of human wishes and needs. Thus they were, in this sense, "atheists." In denying the gods, however, they boldly affirmed faith in the living, active God of heaven and earth.

We uphold faith in the living God only as we continually struggle against the gods (or distorted views of God) that we form in our own image. This struggle will not cease, for we are constantly prone to form God in our own image. We never finish learning and relearning what it means to understand God in light of the Crucified One rather than on the basis of the idols of human reason and imagination.

With this struggle in view, I turn now to two things that most clearly set the living God apart from the gods. First, the living God, in contrast to the gods, acts in mighty ways, doing what appear to human beings as impossibilities. Second, the living God loves people to such an extent that he becomes vulnerable to them, in the process embracing pathos and suffering.

The Living God: Doing Impossibilities

Faced with the powerful allure of other gods throughout its history, Israel countered with the bold assertion of God's incomparability. The Song of Miriam contains one of the earliest expressions of this theme:

> Who is like thee, O Lord, among the gods?
> Who is like thee, majestic in holiness,
> terrible in glorious deeds, doing wonders (or impossibilities)?
> (Ex. 15:11)

Later hymns in Israel's tradition extol God in the same way:

> Thou hast multiplied, O Lord my God,
>   thy wondrous deeds and thy thoughts toward us;
> none can compare with thee! (Ps. 40:5)

> I will call to mind the deeds of the Lord;
>   yea, I will remember thy wonders of old.
> I will meditate on all thy work,
>   and muse on thy mighty deeds.
> Thy way, O God, is holy.
>   What god is great like our God?
> (Ps. 77:11-13; cf. 89:6-7)

Here we see *praise* joined together with *polemic*. Extolling and praising the living God means insisting on the uniqueness of Yahweh over against every other conception of the divine.[18]

But what, we must ask, makes it possible for Israel to assert the incomparability of God over against all other gods? The answer lies in this: the people of Israel, time and again throughout their history, experienced God as the one who does "impossibilities," who performs "wondrous deeds," who shatters conventional assessments of worldly possibility. They saw God work in ways that they could not have imagined or predicted. Out of such experience arose their faith in the God who does impossible things. And out of such experience, therefore, flowed praise to the incomparable one.

Israel's encounter with the God who does "impossibilities" began with the strange episode in Genesis 18:1-15. There the Lord asks Abraham, "Is anything too hard (impossible) for the Lord?" (vs. 14).[19] This question and this text are particularly important, for Scripture keeps returning to it, asking the question in new situations and thereby repeatedly challenging limited human (or secular) conceptions of what is possible. This text, Walter Brueggemann argues, begins an important trajectory or theme running through Scripture. In this trajectory we discover something extremely important about the living God and the perpetual contest with idols.[20]

Remember the story of Abraham up to this point (Gen. 12-17). The Lord has covenanted with Abraham, promising to make of him a great nation. Acting in faith, Abraham has left Haran for Canaan as the Lord directed. Time has passed and he wonders about Sarah's childlessness. He wonders if perhaps Eliezer, a slave born in his household, will have to serve as the heir. But the Lord says, "No, it will be your own son."

More time passes, and Sarah's handmaid bears a son, Ishmael. Sarah, however, remains childless. Abraham turns ninety-nine and the Lord reaffirms the promise, this time specifying that Sarah's son will be named Isaac. Abraham falls on his face and laughs at the very idea.

Then comes the key episode in Genesis 18. The Lord, in the form of three men (angels), appears to Abraham and Sarah by the oaks of Mamre. With great haste Abraham welcomes the three strangers outside the tent, washes their feet, prepares them a full meal, then stands beside them under the tree while they eat (vss. 1-8). The rapid sequence of active verbs in the narrative suggests that "Abraham holds the initiative, administers his life and knows what is possible."

But then the narrative abruptly shifts (vss. 9-15). The three men take the lead, and Abraham must simply listen. They begin probing with a strange power and authority. They ask an abrupt question: "Where is Sarah your wife?" "In the tent," Abraham answers tersely. Then suddenly it is the Lord speaking: "Sarah your wife shall have a son" (vs. 10). Inside the tent Sarah overhears these words. She's ninety years old, and so she laughs to herself at such an outlandish idea. The Lord hears her silent laughter and challenges it with a brusque rebuke: "Why did she laugh?" (vs. 13). In fear now, Sarah denies that she laughed. The Lord insists that she did. And with that the strangers leave and the episode ends.

Abraham and Sarah are simply left with the staggering promise of a child in their old age. And in response to Sarah's laugh, they are left with a staggering question: "Is anything impossible for the Lord?" That promise and that question assault their taken-for-granted world. The ones who administered their lives and knew what was possible and what was not (vss. 1-8) now must wait before the possibility of a new reality beyond conventional definitions of reality (vss. 9-15).

With the birth of Isaac (21:1-3) the promise is fulfilled and the question receives a partial answer. But the question itself—"Is anything impossible for the Lord?"—remains open, its full answer far from clear. For in reality it asks about the freedom of God over against all human formulations of the possible.

In the biblical trajectory where this questions recurs, we find that it always appears radical. For time and again Israel adopts conventional views of what is possible, forgetting that Yahweh, unlike the gods, does "impossibilities." They domesticate God, thinking that God can operate only within the bounds set by human calculation. So the raising of the question, "Is anything impossible for the Lord?" time and again shatters the constricted view of who God is and what God can do.

The story of Samson's birth (Jdgs. 13:12-24) provides one example. This story, like the one in Genesis 18, focuses on the issue of barrenness. An angel of the Lord appears to Manoah's wife, who is barren, and announces that she will bear a son (vss. 2-3). The angel later appears to Manoah, and Manoah, not knowing that he confronts an angel, asks his name. The angel replies that his name is "Impossible" ("Wonderful" in the RSV, vs. 18). Manoah then praises the Lord as the "one who does impossibilities" (or "works wonders," vs. 19).

In this case, it appears, the impossibility wrought by God is twofold. First, a barren woman bears a child, thus reflecting God's earlier blessing of Sarah. But second, as the larger context of this story suggests, God will work through this "impossible" child to free Israel from Philistine oppression. Given Israel's prevailing view of how the world worked, both of these things—the birth of the child and the liberation of Israel—seemed impossible. But God sends a messenger named "Impossible" and announces a new and larger possibility.

Consider another, much later time in Israel's history where our question gets asked again. Jeremiah 32:16-35 records it. Here Jerusalem stands on the verge of destruction by the Babylonians. Jeremiah receives the word of the Lord: "Behold, I am the Lord, the God of all flesh; is anything impossible for me?" (vs. 27). As in Genesis 18:14, the question is rhetorical. But here it concerns not birth, deliverance, and blessing but destruction. For the question stands at the beginning of a long speech announcing the complete destruction of Jerusalem. The "impossibility" wrought by God will be the end of Judah. According to the official theology, however, such an end was simply unthinkable. It was not an option in their catalogue of possibilities. God could never do such a thing to his chosen people.

In the same text Jeremiah transforms God's question into a bold assertion of praise. "Ah Lord God!" he prays. "It is thou who hast made the heavens and the earth by thy great power and by thy outstretched arm! Nothing is impossible for thee. . . ." (vs. 17). He proceeds to review the mighty acts and graciousness of God throughout Israel's past (vss. 17-25). His point is this: God can restore what seems unrestorable. God can renew what appears irretrievably lost. God can begin a new Israel out of the ruins of the old.

As Brueggemann points out, God's question (vs. 27) and Jeremiah's assertion (vs. 17), taken together, indicate two "impossibilities": God can bring an end to what people think they cannot live without, and God can do new things beyond our imagining.

When we follow this theme into the Psalms, we find that it undergirds much of Israel's praise. The psalmists often recite God's mighty and unexpected deeds on behalf of his people. In so doing they sing what one scholar has called "songs of impossibilities."[21] For example:

> We will not hide them from their children,
>   but tell to the coming generation
> the glorious deeds of the Lord, and his might,
>   and the impossibilites (or wonders) which he
>   has wrought.
> In the sight of their fathers he wrought marvels
>   in the land of Egypt, in the fields of Zo'an.
> He divided the sea and let them pass through it,
>   and made the waters stand like a heap.
> In the day time he led them with a cloud,
>   and all the night with a fiery light
>   (Ps. 78:4, 12-14. Cf. Ps. 72:18; 98:1; 139:14).

These "songs of impossibility" celebrate God's surprising reversal of the way things are:

> He raises the poor from the dust,
>   and lifts the needy from the ash heap,
> to make them sit with princes,
>   with the princes of his people.
> He gives a barren woman a home,
>   making her the joyous mother of children.
> Praise the Lord! (Ps. 113:7-9).

These songs assert that what appears downright laughable from a human perspective (remember Sarah in Genesis 18:12) all become possible when God goes to work.

Israel's grave danger—and ours—lies in forgetting the wonders God wrought in the past. Forgetting past "impossibilities" means settling for the way things are. It means reducing life to equations, to what can be predicted, managed, and thus controlled. It means, in many cases, the fashioning of idols. This was Israel's recurring problem.

> They forgot what he had done,
>   and the impossibilities (or miracles) that he had
>   shown them. . . .
> In spite of all this they still sinned;
>   despite his impossibilities (or wonders) they did
>   not believe
>   (Ps. 78:11, 32).

> Our fathers, when they were in Egypt,
>   did not consider your impossibilities (or wonderful
>   works);
> they did not remember the abundance of thy
>   steadfast love (Ps. 106:7. Cf. Jer. 2:5-6 and Neh. 9:17).

Those who do remember, however, discover powerful reasons for praise:

> O give thanks to the Lord, call on his name,
>   make known his deeds among the peoples!
> Sing to him, sing praises to him,
>   tell of all his impossible works! (Ps. 105:1-2).

Those who remember past "impossibilities" can trust in God for new ones. They can open themselves to wonders not yet imagined.

We must now see how this trajectory focusing on God's "impossibilities" that began in Genesis 18:1-15 extends into the New Testament. Three episodes in the Gospels are particularly important.

First is the angel's announcement to Mary of Jesus' birth (Lk. 1:26-38) and Mary's song that follows (1:46-55). After the announcement the angel Gabriel says, "And behold, your kinswoman Elizabeth in her old age has also conceived a son; and this is the sixth month with her who was called barren. For with God nothing will be impossible" (vss. 36-37). Later, when Mary visits Elizabeth, she sings one of those "songs of impossibility," extolling God for his unexpected reversals of the human order of things:

He has put down the mighty from their thrones,
and exalted those of low degree;
he has filled the hungry with good things,
and the rich he has sent empty away (vss. 52-53).

Elizabeth's pregancy and Mary's song both point to the radical "impossibilities" brought to light by the gospel. Here the question asked of Abraham and Sarah so long before, and asked time and again throughout Israel's tradition, receives a full answer.

A second text appears at Mark 10:17-31. To a rich man seeking eternal life Jesus says, "Go, sell what you have, and give to the poor, and you will have treasure in heaven" (vs. 21). In response the man's face falls and he goes sadly away. We know Jesus' famous reply: "Children, how hard it is to enter the Kingdom of God! It is easier for a camel to go through the eye of a needle than for a rich man to enter the kingdom of God" (vss. 24-25).

What we have not been able to hear so well is the response. In astonishment the disciples ask, "Then who can be saved?" Jesus replies, "With men it is impossible, but not with God; for all things are possible with God" (vs. 27). With our "scientific" reading of the Bible, we among Churches of Christ have found it difficult to hear Jesus' response. The "analytic-technical" mindset (as we saw in chapter two) demands an explanation. One must rationalize the metaphor and find "the point." So Campbell (and many of his spiritual descendents) "explained" it:

> The plundering Arabs commonly ride into houses, and commit acts of violence; on this account doors were made low, frequently not more than three feet high. Those who keep camels, and want to introduce them into the courtyard, find this a great inconvenience. To surmount this, they train their camels to fall on their knees while they unload them, and often succeed in teaching them to pass through these low doors on their knees. This was considered a great difficulty; and, therefore, gave rise to the proverb of the camel passing through the needle's eye.[22]

With this explanation, Jesus' wild and shattering metaphor becomes a word of common sense wisdom: salvation is very hard for the rich person, but if he humbles himself and tries hard enough, he can squeeze through the door into heaven.

Such explanation misses entirely the impact of Jesus' words. Read in light of the trajectory we have traced, Jesus' point is inescapable: the kingdom requirement is "impossible," as impossible as the birth of a baby to Sarah, to Manoah's wife, to Elizabeth, or to Mary. Life in the kingdom involves a shattering of the settled, predictable, well-managed, "possible" world.

A third text centers on Jesus' well-known saying about faith: "For truly, I say unto you, if you have faith as a grain of mustard seed, you will say to this mountain, 'Move from here to there,' and it will move; and nothing will be impossible to you" (Matt. 17:21). Here again, as with Abraham and Sarah, faith involves reliance on God's impossible promises. It involves a radical break with what the world tells us is possible and an openness to "impossibilities."

But here we must notice something important throughout this whole biblical trajectory. God does not bring about just any "impossibility." God does not hand people a blank check or say, "Write your own ticket." One cannot seize upon God's promise of "impossibilities" as a kind of blank check offering money, happiness, healing, or whatever else one's heart may desire. That is the way of self-seeking, the way of manipulating God to serve human interests. That, as we have seen, is the way of idolatry.

God's "impossibilities," in contrast, are different. They are rooted in and bounded by God's incomparable character and purpose, not in human desires and wishes. Notice Matthew 17:21 again. It states bluntly that "nothing will be impossible to you," but then, remarkably, the next verse sharply qualifies it: "As they were gathering in Galilee, Jesus said to them, 'The Son of man is to be delivered into the hands of men, and they will kill him, and he will be raised on the third day'" (vs. 22). This juxtaposition of verses suggests that one of the great "impossibilities" of the gospel comes precisely in brokenness, suffering, and death.

Jesus' prayer in Gethsemane makes this particularly clear: "Abba, Father, all things are possible to thee; remove this cup from me; yet not what I will, but what thou wilt" (Mk. 14:36). Here Jesus is clearly a child of that venerable tradition which asks, "Is anything impossible for the Lord?" And Jesus knows the answer. So he prays for the "impossible": the removal of the cup of suffering.

But in Mark's narrative the crucifixion swiftly follows (vss. 43ff.). Jesus drinks the cup. As he does, the point seems clear: the one thing that God cannot or will not do is bestow salvation without death or work deliverance without suffering.

Throughout their long history, the people of God triumphed in the perpetual contest with idols only as they remembered Yahweh's "impossibilities," made them the substance of their praise, and thereby opened themselves in faith to new "impossibilities."

The Living God: Embracing Pathos

God's incomparability lies not only in the fact that he does "impossibilities," but also in the kind of love for his people he displays. Scripture links the two closely together: God performs wonderful, unexpected deeds because of his great love and compassion.

> Let them thank the Lord for his steadfast love,
>   for his wonderful (impossible) works to the sons of
>   men! (Ps. 107:8, 15, 31).
> To him alone who does great wonders (impossibilities),
>   for his steadfast love endures forever;. . .
> to him who divided the Red Sea in sunder,
>   for his steadfast love endures forever;
> and made Israel pass through the middle of it,
>   for his steadfast love endures forever;. . .
> It is he who remembered us in our low estate,
>   for his steadfast love endures forever;
> and rescued us from our foes,
>   for his steadfast love endures forever
>   (Ps. 136:4, 13-14, 23-24).

If God's wonderful and surprising deeds point to the divine loftiness or transcendence, God's steadfast love reveals the divine nearness or immanence.[23] The wonder of all wonders is that the holy and transcendent God draws near to his people. As the prophets put it, God is "the Holy One *in your midst*" (Hos. 11:9; Isa. 12:6; Ezek. 20:41). Moved by love, God comes near, seeking relationship with his people. God becomes vulnerable to them, delighting in their responsiveness to his love, grieving with them in their grief, longing for them in their waywardness, feeling with them when judgment must be carried out. If God appears incomparable in the "impossibilities" he performs, God appears even more incomparable in his loving (and suffering) presence.

Such a conception of God challenges the conception of God held in classical theism. In classical theism God is a philosophical abstraction—unchanging, immovable, passionless, and remote. Aristotle for example spoke of God as the Unmoved Mover, a supremely perfect being who sets the world in motion but remains wholly unmoved by it.

Influenced by such Greek ideas, many early Christian theologians adopted the idea that the perfect divine being cannot suffer. If the God of Scripture was the one absolutely perfect being, they reasoned, then God could not be affected or changed by any outside influence. God therefore could not suffer, for suffering meant vulnerability and vulnerability was a mark of imperfection. This view has shaped much Christian thinking about God down to the present time.[24]

In sharp contrast to the God of classical theism, the God revealed in Scripture is a God who becomes vulnerable to his people. He loves with a passion. He takes risks, exposing his grief and suffering over the waywardness of his beloved. By sharing that suffering, he hopes to touch them deeply and stir them to repentance. And if in their hardness of heart the people are not moved to repent, then at least they will see the pain and agony that judgment causes in the heart of God.

What does this divine vulnerability say about the relationship of God to his people? It says that God in the divine sovereignty limits himself in certain ways for the sake of the relationship. According to Terence Fretheim, God's self-limitation

> might be described as a divine kenosis, a self-emptying, an act of self-sacrifice. The very act of creation thus might be called the beginning of the passion of God. God has so entered the world that God cannot but be affected by its life, including its sinful life. Because this condescending God fully relates to sinful creatures with integrity, and with the deepest possible love, God cannot but suffer, and in manifold ways.[25]

Here is a striking and, for some of us, perhaps a revolutionary insight into the God revealed in the Old Testament. We see nothing less than a God who chooses to share in the human condition, one who humbles himself and becomes vulnerable to us, in all our weakness. We see a God who is nothing less than the Father of Jesus Christ the Crucified One, a God who throughout the ages has experienced something of the pain he endured in the death of his son on the cross.

When we explore those Old Testament texts that speak directly of the divine suffering, we find at least three basic aspects of it.[26] First, God suffers *because* of the people's rejection of him as Lord. The language of divine grief often expresses this suffering.

> How often they rebelled against him in the wilderness
>   and grieved him in the desert!
> They tested him again and again,
>   and provoked the Holy One of Israel (Ps. 78:40-41).

Isaiah says that "in all their affliction he was afflicted" (63:9). The context of both passages implies that God's grieving, though deep and wrenching, does not mean that he is embittered by it or overcome by it. Rather, through it all the divine love and purpose remain constant.

God's suffering because of the people's rejection is tied closely to God's memory. God remembers how things used to be, and yet sees clearly how it all has changed. The past impinges painfully upon the present, and God shares those painful memories with his people:

> I remember the devotion of your youth,
>   your love as a bride,

how you followed me in the wilderness,
in a land not sown (Jer. 2:2).

Here the memories of how the relationship used to be make the present experience of rejection all the more painful. And in the chapters that follow, this grief, deepened by memories, underlies the divine oracles.

In Jeremiah 3, for example, God speaks out of deep pathos:

'I thought
how I would set you among my sons,
and give you a pleasant land,
a heritage most beauteous of all nations.
And I thought you would call me, My Father,
and would not turn from following me.
Surely, as a faithless wife leaves her husband,
so have you been faithless to me, O house of Israel'
(Jer. 3:19-20).

Here God is like a person rejected, not only by his spouse, but by his children as well. God suffers deeply *because* of his people's rejection.

Second, God suffers *with* his suffering people. Though rejection breaks God's heart, God does not desert his people, but immediately returns to them to share their suffering.

For a brief moment I forsook you,
but with great compassion I will gather you.
In overflowing wrath for a moment,
I hid my face from you,
But with everlasting love I will have compassion on you,
says the Lord, your Redeemer (Isa. 54:7-8).

Several texts indicate that God's pain lies not just in the people's rejection of him but also in the suffering such rejection has brought them.

Is Ephraim my dear son?
Is he my darling child?
For as often as I speak against him,
I do remember him still.

> Therefore my heart yearns (or moans) for him;
> I will surely have mercy on him, says the Lord
> (Jer. 31:20).

God never remains indifferent to what has happened to his people. God never feels any satisfaction that justice has been done. For God immediately turns from being judge to being fellow-sufferer. He embraces their suffering, working from within their grief and pain, not just from outside it.

Third, God suffers *for* his broken and suffering people. Here we encounter the most difficult texts—ones that speak of vicarious suffering or divine atonement. Several passages speak of God as the one on whom the people unload their sins.

> I have not burdened you with offerings,
> or wearied you with frankincense.
> But you have burdened me with your sins,
> you have wearied me with your iniquities
> (Isa. 43:23-24).

Here God is said to be loaded down with their sins. By carrying their sins on his own shoulders, as it were, and by holding back the judgment they deserve, God chooses to suffer for them. The cost for God was the expending of the divine life—a concept expressed in the Old Testament through the image of "weariness" (Isa. 1:14; 7:13; Mal. 2:17). In allowing himself to be wearied, God gives up something of the divine life for the purpose of Israel's salvation.

In demonstrating such vulnerability, such suffering love to his people, the living God stands utterly apart from "the gods" of human imagination. God's people triumphed in the relentless contest with idols when they acknowledged this incomparable love and sought to return it.

Conclusion

In this chapter I have traced the history of the contest with idols in Scripture and explored the dynamics of idolatry in our lives. I emphasized that idolatry, at its core, is a religious disguise for self-centeredness and that, for this reason, we are always susceptible to forming God in our own image. I insisted that the idolatrous impulse works even through our most cherished convictions and noblest efforts.

Then, I pointed to two features that most clearly set the living God apart from our many gods: (1) the fact that Yahweh does "impossibilities," thereby shattering our small, narrow, and self-serving conceptions of reality; and (2) the fact that Yahweh loves his creatures even to the point of becoming vulnerable to them and embracing their pain and suffering.

Idolatries of various sorts easily arise when we lose a deep sense of the divine mystery and elusiveness. As we saw in chapters two and three, however, the age in which our movement was born was an age in which God became less mysterious and more predictable. The theology of our own movement, as a result, retained little place for mystery.

Robert Richardson, Alexander Campbell's close friend and associate, speaks the needed word to us about the place and importance of mystery in our faith. His voice was decidedly a minority voice in our heritage—and on this matter almost a lone voice. "What we have fully explored and comprehended," he wrote in his devotional guide of 1888, "wearies us by familiarity, and loses its attractive charm. But mystery awakens curiosity; engages attention; excites inquiry; gives activity to the thought and zest to enjoyment. How just, then, that the most important things should be the most mysterious!"

He then addressed those who feared that mystery served only to block one's vision of spiritual things:

> In proportion as the mysteries presented to us deepen, they approach nearer to God. He is the great mystery of mysteries, and we draw nearer to Him as we approach the veil that conceals the sacred arcana of His inner temple. . . . It is untrue, then, that a mystery that is truly divine, can obstruct our progress or hinder our vision. On the contrary, it tends to give us truer and nobler views of the Deity, because it brings us nearer to Him and yet veils that dazzling glory which would otherwise blind our feeble vision.[27]

Only such a sense of the divine mystery will keep in check our inordinate tendency to bring God within our control and thus to create idols fashioned in our own image.

Notes

Epigraphs: H. Richard Niebuhr, in *The Church Against the World* (Chicago, Ill.: Willett, Clark, 1935), p. 126; C. F. D. Moule, *The Meaning of Hope* (Philadelphia, Pa.: Fortress, 1963), p. 9.

[1] Alexander Campbell, "The Ordinances," *Millennial Harbinger*, New Series, 7 (January 1843):9.

[2] On these two factors see Leonard Allen and Richard Hughes, *Discovering Our Roots: The Ancestry of Churches of Christ* (Abilene, Tex.: ACU, 1988), chapters 4, 5, and 7.

[3] On Israel's polemic against "other gods," see Jon D. Levenson, *Sinai and Zion: An Entry into the Jewish Bible* (New York: Harper & Row, 1987), pp. 56-70.

[4] Otto Baab, *The Theology of the Old Testament* (Nashville, Tenn.: Abingdon, 1949), p. 105.

[5] On Paul and the early Christian encounter with idolatry, see Robert M. Grant, *Gods and the One God* (Philadelphia, Pa: Westminster, 1986), pp. 19-28, 45-53.

[6] H. Richard Niebuhr, *Christ and Culture* (New York: Harper & Row, 1951), p. 155. See also Niebuhr, "Faith in Gods and in God," in *Radical Monotheism and Western Culture* (New York: Harper & Brothers, 1960), pp. 114-26.

[7] Charles L. Loos, "Glorying in the Cross Only," in *The Living Pulpit of the Christian Church*, ed. W. T. Moore (Cincinnati, Ohio, 1868), pp. 457-58.

[8] Ibid., pp. 460-63.

[9] Walter Brueggemann, *The Prophetic Imagination* (Philadelphia, Pa.: Fortress, 1978), pp. 30-37.

[10] Ibid., p. 34.

[11] See Thomas V. Peterson, *Ham and Japheth: The Mythic World of Whites in the Antebellum South* (Metuchen, N.J.: Scarecrow, 1978). For southern preachers' appeals to primitive Christianity in their defense of slavery, see Richard Hughes and Leonard Allen, *Illusions of Innocence: Protestant Primitivism in America, 1630-1875* (Chicago, Ill.: University of Chicago, 1988), chapter 9.

[12] Donald G. Mathews, *Religion in the Old South* (Chicago, Ill.: University of Chicago, 1977), pp. 185-236, and Albert Raboteau, *Slave*

Religion: The Invisible Institution in the Antebellum South (New York: Oxford University, 1978), pp. 211-88. For a case study of these dynamics in more recent times, see Andrew M. Manis, *Southern Civil Religions in Conflict: Black and White Baptists and Civil Rights, 1947-1957* (Athens, Ga.: University of Georgia, 1987).

[13]On the idolatrous mixing of Christianity, capitalism, and American nationalism, see H. Richard Niebuhr, *The Church Against the World*, pp. 128-39; Robert Jewett, *The Captain America Complex: The Dilemma of Zealous Nationalism* (Philadelphia, Pa.: Westminster, 1973); and Robert T. Handy, *A Christian America: Protestant Hopes and Historical Realities*, 2nd. ed. (New York: Oxford University, 1984).

[14]Religious beliefs and symbols, according to Durkheim, are the means by which members of a society "represent to themselves the society of which they are members, and the obscure but intimate relations they have with it." Emile Durkheim, *The Elementary Forms of the Religious Life* (1915; reprint ed., New York: Free Press, 1965), p. 257.

[15]Ludwig Feuerbach, *The Essence of Christianity*, trans. George Eliot (New York: Harper & Row, 1957), p. 73; Hans Küng, *Does God Exist? An Answer for Today*, trans. Edward Quinn (Garden City, N.Y.: Doubleday, 1980), pp. 191-216.

[16]Küng, *Does God Exist?*, pp. 226-36.

[17]Sigmund Freud, *The Future of an Illusion*, trans. W. D. Robson-Scott (London, Eng.: Hogarth, 1928); Joachim Scharfenberg, *Sigmund Freud and His Critique of Religion* (Philadelphia, Pa.: Fortress, 1987).

[18]For an indepth treatment of this theme, see C. J. Labuschagne, *The Incomparability of Yahweh in the Old Testament* (Leiden, Holl.: E. J. Brill, 1966).

[19]The Hebrew word *pela'* has been translated in various ways—"too hard," "extraordinary," "difficult," or "impossible." The rendering "impossible," followed here, seems to catch the intended force of the text. See the discussion by R. Albertz in *Theologisches Handworterbuch zum Alten Testament*, ed. Ernst Jenni (München, 1976), 2:414-20.

[20]I am indebted in this section to Walter Brueggemann, "'Impossibility' and Epistemology in the Faith Tradition of Abraham and Sarah (Gen. 18:1-15)," *Zeitschrift für die Alttestamentliche Wissenschaft* 94 (1982):615-34.

[21]Ibid, p. 623. See also Brueggmann, *Israel's Praise: Doxology against Idolatry and Ideology* (Philadelphia, Pa.: Fortress, 1988).

[22]Alexander Campbell, *The Sacred Writings of the Apostles and Evangelists of Jesus Christ, Commonly Styled the New Testament* (1826; reprint ed., Nashville, Tenn.: Gospel Advocate, 1954), p. 27.

[23]We must use the terms "transcendence" and "immanence" with some care. People often equate transcendence with divine distance and immanence with divine presence, and that can be misleading. Terence Fretheim helps us speak more biblically: "immanence should be more broadly understood in terms of 'relatedness,' of which presence is a significant component, while transcendence should be stripped of its narrow spatial associations and used to speak of the way the Godness of God manifests itself in this relatedness. . . . the immanence/transcendence polarity is not adequate for talk about divine presence. The God who is present is *both* immanent and transcendent; both are appropriate words for a constant divine state of affairs." *The Suffering of God: An Old Testament Perspective* (Philadelphia, Pa.: Fortress, 1984), pp. 70-71. For a treatment of the biblical terminology, see Werner E. Lemke, "The Near and the Distant God: A Study of Jer. 23:23-24 in its Biblical Theological Context," *Journal of Biblical Literature* 100 (1981):541-55.

[24]See Robert M. Grant, *The Early Christian Doctrine of God* (Charlottesville, Va.: University Press of Virginia, 1966), pp. 111-114, and J. K. Mozeley, *The Impassibility of God: A Study in Christian Thought* (Cambridge, Eng.: Cambridge University, 1926).

[25]Fretheim, *Suffering of God*, p. 58. On this theme see also H. Wheeler Robinson, *The Cross in the Old Testament* (London, Eng.: SCM, 1955), and Jürgen Moltmann, "The Passion of God," in *The Trinity and the Kingdom: The Doctrine of God* (San Francisco, Calif.: Harper & Row, 1981), pp. 21-60.

[26]Ibid., pp. 107-48.

[27]Robert Richardson, *Communings in the Sanctuary* (St. Louis, Mo.: Christian Publishing, 1888), pp. 115-16.

5

The Church
Under the Cross

The cross puts everything to the test.
—*Martin Luther*

*In a world grown complex and weary with a
superstructure of belief and practice, he [Alexander
Campbell] sought a principle, the principle of restoration, to winnow out what was primary and essential to
the Christian life.*
—*Morris A. Eames (1966)*

The most pressing question facing Churches of Christ today is the question, Can we recover the "word of the cross" in its biblical fullness? No other question even comes close to this one.

This question towers above all other questions for at least two reasons. First, as we shall see, "the word of the cross" has been significantly displaced in the history of Churches of Christ. Throughout the four generations since Stone and Campbell we have tended to push the cross into the background and thus to proclaim an anemic and distorted gospel.

Second, we presently live in a culture where Jesus' call to follow the way of the cross has become almost unintelligible. Though Christianity seems to be flourishing, it is a Christianity with little room for the cross. The dominant vision of the good life that holds sway everywhere around us today simply excludes the cross.

In light of our own theological tradition and our present culture, then, can we truly proclaim—or even hear—the New Testament "word of the cross"?

Christians throughout the ages of every place, language, and culture have pointed to the cross as the most fundamental point of reference for Christian faith. They have done so because, as we saw in chapter three, the message of the dying and rising Christ comprises the core message (or apostolic *kerygma*) that underlies the New Testament writings.

In a passage reflecting one of the earliest of all Christian confessions, Paul underscores this core message: "For, first of all, I handed on to you that which I also received, namely that Christ died for our sins according to the scriptures, and that he was buried and that according to the scriptures he was raised on the third day" (1 Cor. 15:34). From the Gospels to Paul to most of the other writings, the cross so permeates the New Testament that it stands as the inescapable center and source of Christian life and identity.

As a result Christian people throughout the ages have readily affirmed the centrality of the cross. They have sung its praises, lifted up its symbol, extolled its benefits. But, at the same time, they have most often removed its scandal. They have cherished its symbol, but shunned its discipline. They have lauded its blessings, but sought to remove its burdens. There has always been something deeply disturbing about the cross, something that deeply offends human pride and achievement, something that insults human self-reliance. And so, while confessing the importance of Jesus' death "for us," Christians have been tempted in many ways to alter the radical message of the cross into something more in harmony with human reason, human sensibilities, and human wishes.

What does it mean for the church to live under the cross? What does it mean to worship a crucified God and for the church to live in this world as a cruciform church? What does it mean, in a secular culture that values nothing so much as comfort and self-fulfillment, to find one's most basic identity in the cross? This chapter addresses these questions.

The Displacement of the Cross

Today, as with Christians in the past, we face on every hand the displacement of the cross as the focal point of Christian life. This displacement occurs, not only in crass and blatant ways, but perhaps most often in subtle and quite pious ways. In this section I examine the subtle but serious displacement of the cross in the heritage of Churches of Christ. Later in this chapter we will examine the blatant and pervasive displacement of the cross in American culture.

In looking at the cross in our own heritage, I begin with Barton Stone and Alexander Campbell. Both men believed that the cross was the central and most important truth of the Christian faith. Though they held somewhat different views, both pondered its meaning deeply and extolled its glories.

In a work published in 1805, Stone extolled the cross as the highest revelation of divine love, a revelation containing such compelling and drawing force that it could dramatically transform the human mind, heart, and will and bring about reconciliation with God. Emphasizing the cross's display of divine love, Stone rejected the idea of wrath as an eternal principle in God (when Scripture spoke of divine wrath, he said, it spoke figuratively about God's abhorrence of sin). Christ did not die as our substitute to placate the divine wrath; Christ, that is, did not die in any way to atone God to human beings but rather human beings to God.[1]

Campbell set forth his view of the atonement in a brief section of his book, *The Christian System*, published in 1835. The brevity of the treatment (about 11 pages out of 313) does not accurately reflect the importance of the atonement in his thinking. Campbell wrote that the doctrine of the cross was "the great central doctrine of the Bible, and the very essence of Christianity"; he said it was "a thing of cardinal value in understanding the scriptures." The cross, he added, "explains all the peculiarities of the Christian system, and of the relation of Father, Son, and Holy Spirit, as far as mortals can comprehend them."[2]

Campbell's view of the atonement centered on the theme of sacrifice (which is not surprising since Hebrews, as we saw in chapter three, seems to have served as the functional center of the New Testament for him). He then focused on the Pauline metaphors of propitiation, reconciliation, expiation, and redemption as explaining how Christ died as our sacrifice. To God, Christ's sacrifice was a propitiation (that is, it enabled God to uphold the divine justice while being merciful to sinners); to the sinner, Christ's sacrifice was a reconciliation (displaying divine love, mercy, and willingness to forgive); in regard to sin, Christ's sacrifice was an expiation (a putting away, a purifying); to the saved, Christ's sacrifice was redemption (the deliverance from sin).[3] Campbell believed that Christ died as our substitute, an appeasement of the divine wrath. Stone, as we have seen, rejected this view.

Between 1840 and 1843 Campbell and Stone discussed these issues in the pages of Campbell's journal, *The Millennial Harbinger*, and Stone's journal, *The Christian Messenger*. The discussion focused on the place of the Old Testament sacrificial system in understanding the atonement and on the issue of substitutionary atonement. The exchanges were mostly good-natured, but near the end each man grew a bit testy and hurled a few barbs at the other. When the discussion was broken off rather abruptly, neither man had substantially changed his position. Along the way both had expressed some concern that such discussion might prove divisive.[4]

The point here is that Stone and Campbell each had a robust doctrine of the atonement, a doctrine each had thought long and hard about, a doctrine each assumed stood at the heart of the Christian faith. Part of the problem, however, proved to be that Campbell too readily assumed that people understood the atonement and that the major challenge at hand was restoring "the ancient order of things." He assumed the central doctrine of the Christian faith—the atoning death of Christ—and focused his energies on what he took to be the great challenge of the day: calling people into Christian union on the basis of the ancient order.

Consider in this regard Campbell's advice to young preachers in 1829. Campbell pointed out that preachers should not spend their time teaching people what they already knew. Preachers rather should focus on "reformation," on setting in order the things that remained in disarray. "It is almost universally taken for granted," Campbell told them, "that the audience believes that there is a God, a Saviour, a judgement, a heaven, a hell." Preachers, he added, could almost always assume this much about their congregations. They could assume it because "mothers, fathers, uncles, aunts, or some other benevolent being, nurse guardian, schoolmaster, or other, had planted these seeds before the preacher ever addressed them from his sacred tub." Basic things like the atonement people learned from parents and others, so much so that "we address a people acknowledging all of the great cardinal facts and truths of Christianity." Young preachers should acknowledge this and focus on "reformation" and gospel order.[5]

Here we find an important clue to the displacement of the cross in our movement. Assuming a basic grasp of the atonement and its meaning for Christian faith, our movement became preoccupied with form, structure, and the setting in order of what was lacking. The "word of the cross," in its New Testament fullness, was partially displaced.

To understand this displacement more fully, however, we must look deeper. We must look again at the way of reading the Bible that became a powerful tradition in the movement. We must recall some of the key points developed earlier in chapters two and three. There I described the new scientific view of the world that emerged in the eighteenth century and the "analytic-technical mindset" it produced. Moved by enormous confidence in the power of human reason to manage and control the world, this mindset sought hard facts and precisely stated propositions. It sought formulas and equations whereby one might exercise ever greater control over the world.

This mindset, as it was applied to the Bible in the eighteenth and early nineteenth centuries, produced an unprecedented literalism. People increasingly read the Bible as a collection of precisely stated propositions or facts. The Baconian method of scientific induction, having wrought wonders in the realm of natural science, was widely adopted as the only true method of reading the Bible.

As we saw in chapter two, this Baconian scientific approach to scripture brought problems, especially as it hardened and became more cut-and-dried in the generations after

Campbell. In regard to the atonement, this approach to the Bible presented at least three closely related problems. First, this approach tended to level the New Testament into a collection of doctrinal facts. The cross was one of these facts, important to be sure, but only one fact among many others in the New Testament pattern.

Second, this approach, like the scientific spirit of the age, had little patience with mystery, seeking instead what was practical, useful, and subject to human mastery. Thus, as numerous preachers clearly asserted, engaging the mysteries and profundities of the atonement held little practical value. The surpassing question was simply, "What must I do to be saved?" The cross was simply a historical fact; one should believe that fact, then concentrate on one's proper response to it.

Third, with its focus on precise fact, this approach proved unable to take proper account of narrative and the language of metaphor. As we have seen, those who employed this method insisted that narratives and metaphorical language be "rendered simple," or reduced to precise, factual language. Metaphors were too imprecise, too laden with mystery, too resistant to formulaic control. Metaphorical language was sloppy and did not carry the weight of fact.

The New Testament, however, conveys the significance of the atonement primarily through narrative and rich metaphor. The New Testament writers do not primarily offer formal dogmatic assertions or definitions. For them, the cross is not simply a fact. Rather, they tell the story and employ a series of images or word pictures (metaphors). They speak of conflict and victory, vicarious suffering, sacrifice, ransom and redemption, reconciliation, justification, and adoption, among others.

These terms go beyond purely factual language; they are expansive word pictures which point to and illumine a transcendent reality always larger than the terms themselves. They are windows into a divine transaction whose meaning can never be exhausted in human language. They function to draw us into that unfathomable reality, seeking always to deepen our sense of the divine holiness, mercy, and love revealed in it. Aversion to metaphor quickly reduces and displaces the New Testament "word of the cross."

Another factor in our traditional approach to the Bible which contributed to the displacement of the cross was the dispensational arrangement of Scripture. As we saw in chapter three, the Gospels were relegated to the Mosaic dispensation and thus clearly took a back seat to Acts and the Epistles. Furthermore, the Gospels were used most frequently, not so much to focus on the meaning of Christ's death, but to show how the resurrection proved the proposition that Jesus was the divine Messiah. With this proposition proven, the stage was then set for the central event—the beginning of God's kingdom and the coronation of Jesus as king (Acts 2). It became commonplace in the movement to point to Acts 2 as the center of the Bible, as the heart of God's plan, rather than to the event of the cross narrated in the gospels.[6]

The displacement of the cross brought about by this method of reading the Bible was subtle at first. But as time passed the displacement grew more noticeable and, at times, striking.

Consider for example John Sweeney's sermon entitled "What Must I Do To Be Saved?" In this sermon he stated in no uncertain terms why he opposed spending much time exploring the meaning of atonement. The question, "What must I do to be saved?" he insisted,

> ...is a practical question. It is the practical question, and, in fact, the only really practical question in the whole matter of our salvation. Of course, God saves us. His love is the prime moving cause of our salvation.... The death of Jesus is the sole meritorious, or compensative cause of our salvation. But even the atonement is not a practical question.... How the death of Christ met the demands of justice and satisfied the claim of the Law against us, is not a practical question. It is enough for us to accept the facts as stated in the word of God.... It is not what must God, or Christ, or the Holy Spirit do? But what must I do? That's the practical question with us in the whole matter."[7]

Sweeney's rationale for preaching the gospel reflects a decided tendency in the movement. There was affirmation of the fact of the atonement but reluctance to delve much into its meaning. Thus preachers could preach sermons entitled, "What Must I Do To Be Saved?" and scarcely even mention the crucifixion or atonement of Christ.[8]

One of the most striking examples of the displacement of the cross appears in T. W. Brents' huge volume, *The Gospel Plan of Salvation* (1874). It became a standard work and was widely read for decades (by 1950 it had gone through thirteen editions). The only extended treatment of the atonement is a five-page section devoted to refuting the Calvinistic doctrine of limited atonement. Although one finds a few references to Christ's death scattered throughout the book's 662 pages, nowhere does one find any systematic or extended discussion of human need and how God met that need at the cross. Brents devotes 306 pages to a discussion of baptism. But even there I found only about two pages even connecting baptism to the death of Christ.[9] In a book claiming to set forth the gospel plan of salvation, I find such omission astounding, the sign of something deeply awry in the theology of the movement.

A recent study by Bill Love provides an illuminating picture of how preachers in our movement have proclaimed the cross. The study surveyed hundreds of books of printed sermons throughout the five generations of Restoration preaching between 1800 and 1950, asking: "What did the people hear from the pulpit? and, Did we preach the 'word of the cross' as Paul did, naturally in every situation?" In each of the five generations, Love selected five of the most influential preachers. In working through all their published sermons, he tallied the number of sermons mentioning the cross and then recorded each time one of the sermons discussed any of six major New Testament metaphors for the atonement.

Some of the study's conclusions are as follows: (1) The New Testament proclaims the atonement naturally in every situation. If it was divided up into sermon-length sections, scarcely a section of the New Testament would fail to make significant reference to the death, burial, and resurrection of Jesus.

(2) Restoration preaching stands in marked contrast. While the first generation of preachers mentioned the cross in about two-thirds of their sermons, succeeding generations mentioned it far less frequently (in the fifth generation, for example, preachers mentioned the cross in only one-third of their sermons).

(3) In general preachers seldom did much substantive exposition of the meaning of the cross. They often mentioned it briefly in the invitation, pointing to it as a proof of God's love. Some preachers said that the atonement should be affirmed but not discussed, since its mysteries easily confused people and exploring such things held no practical value in following the plan of salvation.

(4) The wide range of New Testament pictures (or metaphors) of the cross was lost. When the atonement metaphors were addressed, only two stand out—the metaphors of priest/sacrifice and reconciliation.

(5) When the cross is mentioned the emphasis often falls on the resurrection as a proof of the proposition that Jesus was the Son of God, not on the significance of the death itself.

Bill Love summarizes his study with these words: "What was assumed in the first generation virtually disappears from the second generation on. Where the atonement does appear the concepts are fragmentary and anemic. Ironically for a movement devoted to restoration of the New Testament faith, nothing like the richness of the New Testament doctrine of the atonement appears in our preaching."[10]

In response to this displacement of the cross, we are faced with an enormous and sobering question. It is the question asked by Charles L. Loos in a brief article of 1869 in *The Millennial Harbinger*. Campbell's periodical seldom dealt in depth with the cross, and this article is the only one listed in the index under "cross." In this article Loos asks simply: "What is left of the Gospel, if you take away the cross?"

What is left, Loos answers, is the teaching and example of Christ. But "if Jesus brings us only His doctrine and His example, the Gospel, instead of being the good news, is only, like the Law, an instrument of condemnation and death." For viewing the glorious and perfect life of Jesus and hearing his call to live such a life would only deepen awareness of our failures and make us "feel more grievously than ever our sin and helplessness." We need pardon, deliverance, and empowerment, and through his cross Jesus brings these to us.[11]

It's an eloquent and powerful little article tucked away in one of the last volumes of Campbell's journal. Its central question haunts me: "What is left of the gospel, if you take away the cross?"

In view of the displacement of the cross in the Stone/Campbell movement, I answer that what was left was a distorted and anemic gospel. The gospel of grace became a gospel of duty, law, and perfect obedience. Covenant, we might say, became contract. We have often preached that Christ died as the mediator of a new covenant between God and human beings (Heb. 9:15; 1 Cor. 11:25). But consider the difference between covenant and contract. Though similar in some ways, they differ radically in spirit. A contract defines a precise set of relationships and obligations, and if these are correctly observed then the contractual obligations are fully discharged and the benefits fully received.

But covenant in the biblical sense is far different. In the Old Testament God's steadfast love constantly attempts to win back his people when they have spurned his covenant (Jeremiah 30). Despite Israel's unfaithfulness, God the relentless lover still seeks her out and brings her back (Hos. 2:19-23). Even though Israel forgets its maker and deserves the sentence of exile and even death (Hos. 8:14, 11:5-7), God's compassion will not let him carry out the sentence (11:8-9). Though wounded deeply by Israel's infidelity, God (as we saw in chapter four) withholds judgment as long as possible; but even when judgment finally becomes necessary, God quickly turns from being judge to being fellow-sufferer (Isa. 54:7-8; Jer. 31:20).

God's covenant with people, unlike a contract, always arises out of grace; and it always has a growing edge to it that nourishes rather than limits relationships. Contracts contain little room for slippage; they are legal arrangements that say in essence, "Do your part or else." God's covenants, in contrast, always begin with an act of grace and are deeply personal in nature. They are demanding, to be sure, but because they are rooted in love and trust they contain elements of spontaneous giving and forgiving which permeate the continuing relationship.[12] At the center of the biblical story we find a God who embraces Israel's pain, a God who cares in costly ways. Such caring is precisely what mere contracts cannot do.

As the cross was diminished in our movement, God's gracious and deeply personal covenant, mediated by a stunning display of suffering love, increasingly became a bare contract.

The most common traditional formulation of the gospel reflects this shift. The gospel consisted of three facts to be believed (Christ's death, burial, and resurrection), three commands to be obeyed (believe, repent, and be baptized upon a confession of faith), and three promises to be received (forgiveness of sin, the gift of the Spirit, and hope of eternal life). God had already fulfilled his part of the contract; human beings must now fulfill all their obligations or else the contract was broken. All benefits promised in the contract depended entirely upon the exact fulfillment of all contractual obligations.

By the late nineteenth century this formulation had been well established as orthodoxy in the movement. Occasionally someone questioned the formulation, and the response usually served to underscore how deeply entrenched it was.

Consider an episode in the 1930s involving the Oklahoma preacher K. C. Moser. In 1932 Moser published a small book entitled *The Way of Salvation*. Its central theme was salvation by grace through faith. The conviction that justification comes by faith and not by works permeated it. Moser wrote for example:

> Christ crucified is man's all in all. He kept the Law perfectly, and then, bearing man's iniquities, died on the cross. . . . It means that when man goes to God for mercy he must go pleading the blood of Christ; and when God bestows pardon, He does so out of regard for the atonement made for man by 'His only begotten son,' 'whom He set forth to be a propitiation through faith in His blood.' To man, thus believing in Christ, thus trusting in the blood of Christ, God imputes righteousness. . . . the obedience of Christ becomes the righteousness of the believer. The believer does not have to depend upon his

own imperfect obedience. He pleads the obedience of Christ. Christ is his righteousness.

Moser later asserted that "this divine righteousness should be the theme of every gospel sermon. There is no gospel without it." He added that "a false doctrine of justification is as effective an enemy of Christ as irreligion."[13]

As Richard Hughes recounts the story, Moser's view touched off a furor in the 1930s. He denied the Baconian formulation of the gospel as "facts, commands, or promises." He insisted that the gospel concerns the person of Jesus and trust in him, not mere facts. The gospel, he said, was Jesus Christ crucified, buried, and raised for our deliverance. For such views, Moser drew a storm of attack, so much so that he was barred from participation in most brotherhood events for over forty years.[14]

Moser however was not alone in his concern about the displacement of the cross and of God's grace. In a laudatory review of Moser's book in the *Gospel Advocate*, G. C. Brewer took the opportunity to warn about this tendency in the movement. "Some have been wont to show that there was a human side and a divine side to salvation," Brewer wrote, "and in doing so they have made the *human coordinate with the divine* .... The gospel was made a system of divine laws for human beings to obey and thus save themselves sans grace, sans mercy, sans everything spiritual and divine—except that the 'plan' was in mercy given."[15]

In the years that followed, Brewer repeated his concern about the eclipse of the cross and the overshadowing of grace. In a 1952 lecture on "Grace and Salvation," Brewer again spoke out of grave concern. "Our salvation does not depend upon our perfect adherence to the requirements of law," he said. "By making our salvation dependent upon our own perfection, we make void the grace of God. And to make our perfection a matter of legal requirements fully met would make Christ's death useless (Galatians 2:21; 3:21)."[16]

Both Moser and Brewer saw a serious displacement of the cross in the movement, and both called their sisters and brothers to rethink the traditional formulation of the gospel.

Since their time that rethinking has been taking place, here and there, mostly by fits and starts. It continues today.

For well over 150 years Churches of Christ have called for restoration of New Testament Christianity. It has been a powerful ideal. It has shaped our identity as a movement. The call to restore always resounds as a call back to the center and source of faith. Jesus' death and resurrection stand solidly at the center of that faith. Today we face the continuing challenge of lifting up the cross and restoring it to the central place among us.

The Centrality of the Cross

Restoring the centrality of the cross will mean, as we have seen, appropriating the rich metaphors used by the New Testament writers to provide windows into the meaning of the cross.

These metaphors, we must remember, are not simply facts, not simply propositions that can be assembled like puzzle pieces into a doctrine of the atonement. They are pictures. They are scenes of dark and compelling beauty laid out before us. One does not simply learn them as one might learn a list of definitions. Rather one stands before them, admiring their beauty and pondering their meaning. And though the pictures grow familiar, one returns often to them, for like a great masterpiece in a museum they never seem to be exhaustible or to grow old.

Here I look briefly at seven important New Testament metaphors picturing Christ's death for us.

1) *Suffering Servant*. One of the most important images (and probably the earliest) used to picture the significance of Christ's death was that of the suffering servant figure derived from Isaiah. In a series of Servant Songs (Isa. 42:1-9; 49:1-6; 50:4-11; 52:13-53:12; and possibly 61:1-2), Isaiah presents a vivid picture of Yahweh's chosen servant. God chose this servant as a messenger to the nations. God put the divine Spirit within him so that as the servant faced growing opposition, persecution, and death, he would not grow weary or disheartened in the pursuit of his task.

In carrying out this task, the servant was "wounded for our transgressions" and "bruised for our iniquities" (53:5). He bore the sin of many, and he did it meekly, without resistance, like a lamb led to the slaughter (53:7, 12). God will exalt and prosper his faithful servant, and when he does, kings and nations will be startled by him and drawn to him, acknowledging that "with his stripes they are healed."

This image of the suffering servant becomes fundamentally important in the New Testament. For this is the central image through which Jesus himself understood his Messianic mission. It was the metaphor Jesus himself chose to picture the meaning of his life and death. In announcing his Messianic program, for example, Jesus quotes from one of the Servant Songs (Lk. 4:16-21; Isa. 61:1-2). Matthew's gospel interprets Jesus' ministry of healing and exorcism in reference to Isaiah's picture of the servant (Mt. 8:16-17; Isa. 53:4). When Jesus withdraws from the crowds and maintains a low-key ministry, Matthew explains it by citing another of the Servant Songs (Mt. 12:16-21; Isa. 42:1-4).

In Luke's account Jesus himself refers to the servant picture to interpret his impending death (Luke 22:37), and there are strong echoes of the Servant Songs in Jesus' other allusions to his passion and death (Mk. 8:31; 9:12; 10:33-34, 45; 14:21). This image also appeared in the earliest apostolic preaching (Acts 3:13, 26; 8:32-35) and in primitive Christian hymns (Phil. 2:7; I Peter 2:21-25).[17]

The suffering servant metaphor occupies a particularly important place in understanding Jesus' death. First, it is the imagery that Jesus himself chose. And second, it illumines the vicarious nature of Jesus's death (his death "for us"). Yet, according to the study of five generations of printed sermons in our movement (cited earlier), this metaphor figured significantly in only one sermon.[18]

2) *Conflict and victory.* This metaphor, like that of the suffering servant, is one of the most prominent in the New Testament. In the synoptic Gospels, for instance, Jesus' conflict with an opposing power becomes a key theme. Jesus' conflict with the tempter first sets the stage for his ministry (Mt. 4:1-17). Then throughout his ministry the Gospels depict Jesus as doing

battle with the Evil One. This Evil One rules over a powerful kingdom, disrupting all of creation and holding humankind under his sway (Lk. 11:17,18).

The Gospels further depict Jesus' casting out of evil spirits or demons as victories over this kingdom. These victories mark the rise of a new era of salvation, the dawning of God's kingdom (Mt. 12:28; Lk. 11:20). As Jesus sends out the seventy to proclaim this kingdom, he gives them authority over the powers of evil. And when they return from their mission, Jesus says, "I saw Satan fall like lightning from heaven" (Lk. 10:17-18).

Paul and other early Christian writers develop this conflict image into a major metaphor for understanding the death of Christ. In his death Christ won a shattering victory over the "principalities and powers"—the invisible spiritual forces which oppress and enslave people, which hold people in a grip they cannot break.

Paul speaks of enslavement to the "elemental spirits of the universe" (Gal. 4:3, 9; Col. 2:8, 20). These spirits or powers comprise a field of interlocking forces. Among these powers or elemental spirits Paul includes the law, for it too becomes an enslaving and deceiving power. Sin is another of the powers. It is a power that enslaves, a power Paul can speak of as "reigning and having dominion" over us (Rom. 6:6; 5:14-17, 21). Sin deceives and kills; it makes war and takes captives (Romans 7:11, 23). It is a deadly power which one can overcome only through the "Spirit of life in Christ Jesus" (Romans 8:2). The alliance of sin with the law brings death (Rom. 7:11). Death thus "reigns" as the primal power (Rom. 6:9; 5:17).

The early Christians saw in Jesus' cross the decisive victory over the powers, the climax of the battle that God had been waging over the centuries. Through Jesus' cross God "disarmed the principalities and powers and made a public example of them, triumphing over them in him" (Col. 2:15). Then in raising Christ, God placed him "far above all rule and authority and power and dominion," and "put all things under his feet and has made him the head over all things to the church" (Eph. 1:21-22).[19]

With the rise of the modern worldview, the biblical vision of a realm of invisible enslaving powers gradually has receded, and with it the image of Christ's death as victory over the powers. It seems strange and foreign to many modern people. The minor place of conflict/victory imagery in our own heritage reflects this trend.

3) *Sacrifice.* Although apparently not as prominent in the earliest Christian community as those of suffering servant and conflict/victory, this metaphor became an extremely important way of interpreting Christ's death. The imagery here is complex and varied. Sacrifice imagery in the New Testament depends upon at least three major Old Testament pictures of sacrifice.

First was the sin-offering and atonement ritual performed on the annual Day of Atonement (Leviticus 4 and 16). A person brought an unblemished animal to the altar, laid hands on it (symbolizing identification with the victim), then slaughtered it. The sacrifice was an offering of life to God, a means of making atonement or "covering over" sin (Lev. 17:11). It was the costly act of rendering an impure person acceptable to God and of interrupting the progressive course of evil that sin set in motion.

Second was the sacrifice of the Passover lamb. The blood sprinkled on the doorpost of the house covered or shielded the offerer from the powers of destruction (Ex. 12:22-23).

Third were the sacrifices used to seal the covenant at Sinai (Ex. 24:3-11). Moses read "the book of the covenant" and the people all said, "All that the Lord has spoken we will do, and we will be obedient." Moses then sprinkled the people with blood, saying, "Behold the blood of the covenant which the Lord has made with you."

Paul, in his prominent use of sacrificial imagery, draws especially upon sin-offering and Passover imagery. Paul says that God for our sakes made Christ "to be sin [or a sin offering] who knew no sin, so that in him we might become the righteousness of God" (2 Cor. 5:21; cf. Rom. 8:3; 3:25). Drawing upon another picture of sacrifice, Paul writes that, "Christ, our Passover Lamb, has been sacrificed"; he then admonishes his readers to "celebrate the festival" (1 Cor. 5:7-8).

We find the sacrificial imagery most prominent in Hebrews (8:1-10:18). There Jesus becomes both high priest and sin-offering. With the Day of Atonement ritual as the backdrop, Hebrews pictures Christ, the eternal high priest, entering the sanctuary offering his own blood as a single perfect sacrifice (Heb. 9:6-14). Then, with the Old Testament's covenant sacrifice as the backdrop, the writer pictures Christ as the mediator of a new covenant through the sprinkling of his blood (Heb. 9:15-22; 10:15-18; cf. Mt. 26:28, 1 Cor. 11:25).[20]

The rich and vivid metaphor of sacrifice provides a deep glimpse into the meaning of Christ's death. But this metaphor, like the others, cannot exhaust or adequately define that death.

4) *Ransom and redemption.* This important metaphor pictures the freeing of slaves or the act of deliverance from some kind of bondage. Mixed with other metaphors, it vividly pictured to the primitive Christian community how Jesus' death had freed them from bondage to sin, to Satan, and to the evil powers.

The backdrop for this imagery was provided by God's mighty redemption of Israel from Egyptian bondage (Ex. 6:6; 15:13; Deut. 9:26; 21:8; Micah 6:4). This was the point at which God's saving grace was most sharply focused in the Old Testament. Out of sheer love God chose the people of Israel and redeemed them by his mighty power. God entered into covenant relationship with them and committed himself to being their deliverer. The Old Testament in many ways pictures God as redeeming his people from various forces that threatened them (e.g., Ps. 25:22; 34:22; 49:15; 144:10; Hos. 13:14). God's redemptive acts are pictured not so much as commercial transactions involving payment of a ransom price but rather as free, yet costly acts of divine grace (Isa. 45:13; 52:3).

New Testament writers extend and adapt this Old Testament imagery to understand the meaning of Christ's death. Luke for example asserts that just as the exodus from Egypt required a deliverer, so the new exodus from sin's bondage also requires a deliverer. In this way the role of a redeemer or deliverer, which was God's alone in the Old Testament, was ascribed to Jesus (Acts 7:35; Lk. 21:28; 1:69). This imagery also formed Jesus' own understanding of his mission: "The Son of Man came . . . to give his life a ransom for many" (Mt. 20:28; Mk. 10:45). The ransom image here relates closely to Jesus' use of the suffering servant imagery and is probably based on Isaiah 53:10-12.

In Paul's use of this imagery, he draws on the practice (common in his day) of buying a slave's freedom. He pictures human beings in slavery to sin, to the curse of the law, and to the "elemental spirits of the universe" (Rom. 6:15-23; 7:14; Gal. 3:10-13; 4:3-7). The cost of redemption was the death of the Messiah; by submitting to crucifixion he became a curse on our behalf. As a result of this act, Paul says, people are "made righteous" and set free from bondage to become free children of God (Gal. 3:8-13; 4:57). Elsewhere Paul says, "You were bought with a price" (I Cor. 6:20; 7:23). His point is not so much the size of the price or to whom it was paid, but rather that the price has indeed been paid and redemption completed. Christians therefore belong to Christ, not themselves.[21]

(5) *Reconciliation.* This image pictures the restoring of friendship and peace by the removal of enmity. The term means literally to bring people into council again. Though this image appears only twelve times in five passages (Rom. 5:10-11; 11:15; 2 Cor. 5:17-20; Eph. 2:14-16; Col. 1:19-22), it provides a fundamentally important picture into what Christ accomplished through his death.

Paul's picture of reconciliation emphasizes that God always takes the initiative. Through the cross God graciously takes the initiative to remove the barriers of hostility that people have erected against him. The idea is not that God must be reconciled to human beings, but rather that human beings must be reconciled to God. Through the cross God has done that. "We were reconciled to God through the death of his Son" (Rom. 5:10). Those who "once were far off have been brought near in the blood of Christ" (Eph. 2:13). Through Christ God was at work reconciling all things to himself, "making peace by the blood of his cross" (Col. 1:20).

But the reconciling work of Christ not only brings about peace, it also brings about a substantial change in people. Christ's love becomes a compelling force in people's lives (2 Cor. 5:14). One becomes a "new creation," which means not simply an inward change in one's own life but rather the incorporation into a whole new social reality or order. Steeped as we are in Western individualism, with its preoccupation with personal guilt, introspection, and individual fulfillment, we easily miss the broad scope of this reconciling work. 2 Corinthians 5:17 might best be rendered: "So when anyone is in Christ there is a whole new world, the old order has lost its force, the new one has been created."

God's reconciling work, displayed supremely in the cross, creates a reconciling community, not simply reconciled individuals. Here social distinctions, racial prejudices, and religious advantages begin to break down (Col. 3:10-11). Here truth-telling, sacrificial love, burden-bearing, meekness, and non-violence become the order of the day. Here divine grace spins off into human graciousness. For the cross creates a new social order, God's reconciling community.[22]

(6) *Justification.* This metaphor pictures the work of Christ in a legal or juridical setting. Western Christianity, especially since Martin Luther and the Protestant Reformation, has tended to elevate this metaphor above all others, thus placing more emphasis on it than does Scripture. In this way some of the metaphors that were more central to Jesus and the earliest Christians were eclipsed. Considerable distortion resulted. As one scholar noted, Western Christianity has "poured content into its understanding of the juridical metaphor from the familiar spheres of Roman law (guilt, punishment, satisfaction, acquittal) and Greek philosophy (abstract concept of universal moral law), while the apostles used the juridical metaphor with Old Testament covenant concepts in mind."[23]

This metaphor is rooted in the biblical portrayal of God's justice or righteousness. God revealed his righteousness in the mighty acts by which he delivered Israel and entered into a gracious, personal covenant relationship with them. Thus the righteousness of God refers fundamentally to God's faithfulness to the demands of the covenant relationship. Israel's proper response to God's saving acts (or righteousness) was covenant faithfulness—living in a way that reflects God's righteousness. Because God acts justly (or righteously) human beings must pursue justice (or righteousness).

Micah 6:1-8 states it clearly: having experienced the "saving acts of the Lord," Israel's proper response was "to do justice, and to love kindness, and to walk humbly with . . . God" (6:5, 8). This becomes the biblical model: God performs great deeds of righteousness and calls his covenant people to walk along with him in the way of righteousness.

This covenant relationship, rather than Western legal practices, provides the backdrop for Paul's use of this metaphor. Jesus' faithfulness unto death most clearly and supremely displays the divine righteousness or saving activity (Rom. 1:16-17; 3:21-26; 5:19). But human beings have shown themselves universally unfaithful to God's covenant. Thus they stand condemned before the divine court. Under the divine lawsuit, the world stands guilty, speechless before the divine judgment.

But despite human unfaithfulness God remains faithful. In the cross God stepped in and set things right again. Through the cross God justifies the unrighteous, restoring them into covenant relationship with God and with God's people. But God's act is not simply a legal transaction. It is not simply pronouncing the unrighteous righteous. It is being set right *and* called to the righteous life, the life of covenant faithfulness. It is a call to the "obedience which leads to righteousness" (Rom. 6:16).[24]

(7) *Adoption.* This metaphor pictures Jesus' death as bringing people into God's family. It appears in five New Testament passages (Rom. 8:15; 8:23; 9:14; Gal. 4:4-5; Eph. 1:5-7). One of these passages explicitly relates adoption to Christ's death: "He destined us in love to be his sons through Jesus Christ. . . . In him we have redemption through his blood, the forgiveness of our trespasses according to the riches of his grace" (Eph. 1:5-7). Two other of these passages speak of God as "Abba," emphasizing the depth and intimacy of relationship that Christ's death makes possible (Rom. 8:15-16; Gal. 4:6).

We have looked at seven important pictures held up in the New Testament to convey the meaning of Christ's death. There are a few others, but these are major ones. Through the proliferation of such pictures, the early Christian writers are telling us that no single picture or even a series of pictures can ever contain or fathom the meaning of Christ's death. These pictures permeate the New Testament writings, vividly underscoring for us the centrality of the "word of the cross" in the primitive Christian community.

It is not enough, however, to say that the "word of the cross" pervades the New Testament writings. This pervasiveness might suggest simply that the atonement constitutes one of the important New Testament doctrines. And indeed it does. But it is not simply that. The cross rather provides the lens which focuses the distinctively Christian view of things. It provides the dominant vision of what life in Christ should be like.

Through the lens of the cross, we can say, this dominant vision of reality becomes cruciform or cross-shaped. Consider three ways the cross does this. First, through the cross we see the heart of God revealed most clearly. Second, only through the cross can we see the true nature of human sin and the depths of divine grace. And third, the cross provides the model for God's new social order, the messianic community.

But in shaping this cruciform vision, the cross remains always a stumbling block or scandal (Gal. 5:11). In each of these three areas the cross inevitably proves itself deeply unsettling, deeply threatening. For the cross challenges our favorite conceptions of God. It assaults all human pretensions, all human achievements and wisdom, all reasons for glorying. The cross exposes our God-substitutes, our self-serving religiosity, and breaks through the illusion that we are the masters of our own lives. It challenges the complacency of churches that dare to call themselves by the name of the Crucified One. As Martin Luther once put it, "the cross puts everything to the test."

(1) *The cross reveals the heart of God most clearly, thereby putting all our human conceptions of God to the test.* The cross reveals the depth of God's suffering love. As we saw in chapter four, God revealed himself to Israel as the God who embraces pathos, who in the divine sovereignty limits himself in certain ways for the sake of relationship with his beloved. We saw how the prophets pictured God as the weeping parent or the betrayed husband (Jer. 8:18-19, 21). We saw that even when God must judge Israel, God quickly turns from being judge and be-

comes fellow-sufferer with them, taking their pain up into the divine heart.

At Calvary the cross that had long been planted in the heart of God became stunningly visible for all to see. As C. A. Dismore put it, "there was a cross in the heart of God before there was one planted on the green hill outside of Jerusalem. And now that the cross of wood has been taken down, the one in the heart of God abides, and it will remain so long as there is one sinful soul for whom to suffer."[25]

The cross thereby challenges and breathtakingly alters our human conceptions of what God must be like. We think of God as high and lifted up, enclosed in glory; the cross reveals God as stooping and lowly, enduring shame. We think of God as omnipotent, invulnerable, and unaffected; the cross reveals God as making himself vulnerable because of love, exposing himself to all the world as one who appears weak and powerless. We think of God working his will through sheer almightiness; the cross shows us that God has chosen to work his will through the power of suffering love.

In the presence of the Crucified One "we learn how difficult, how terrible, and how wonderful it is to say that God is love, and that his love is most perfectly revealed on a cross."[26] In that presence we catch glimpses of love's enormous costs, its intense yearnings, its unexpected vulnerability. If the cross provides our clearest glimpse into the heart of God, then we must be prepared to have our cherished notions of God transformed. For the cross puts all our conceptions of God to the test.

(2) *The cross reveals to us the true nature of human sin and the depth of divine grace.* If the cross provides the clearest window into the divine heart, it also provides a window into the labyrinth of the human heart. We do not truly see our sin until we see something of what our sin cost God. We cannot know the extent of our estrangement from God until we see something of the distance God had to travel to reach us. We do not confess our sin, then turn to the cross. Rather we see Jesus lifted up on the cross and find ourselves moved to confess our sin.

The cross therefore is deeply wounding, for it exposes us for what we really are. The cross passes judgment on the prideful human self, for it is that self which presents the greatest obstacle to God's work. The prideful self tends to regard itself as self-sufficient. It is turned in upon itself, sick with spiritual narcissism. We dare not admit the depths of our own inadequacy, the fullness of our need, the extent of our helplessness. The cross pulls out the props from under that self, forcing us to concede our inadequacies so that we may turn to God.

In the light of the cross we begin to see something of the depth and subtlety of sin. We begin to see something of the power of human self-deception. "We will do almost anything," Stanley Hauerwas has written, "to avoid recognizing the limits on our claims to righteousness. In fact, we seem to be able to acknowledge those limits only when life has brought us to the point where we can do nothing else. To accept the gospel is to receive training in accepting the limits on our claims to righteousness before we are forced to. It is a hard and painful discipline. . . ."[27]

Thus the cross puts our lives to the test. Those who call themselves the church gather around that cross and there hear again and again the sobering first word of the gospel—that human beings are deeply sinful, turned in upon themselves, mired in grand illusions. For the cross demands that we face the truth about ourselves: that we are not completely rational, autonomous persons, that we cannot "have it all," that we are not creatures with infinite potential hidden away within ourselves, that we are people of neurotic self-concern, prone to think that our vision of things defines reality.

In the cross we can face the sobering and troubling truth about ourselves because, no matter how deeply it exposes our sin and self-deception, the cross at the same time reveals that God's grace always reaches deeper than our sin. Far deeper. Because it is grace, in fact, there is no telling just how far it reaches. In the cross God's love and mercy meet us at the point of our greatest need, our most shattering failures. Through the cross God says, not "Give me your virtue, give me your goodness, and I will crown it with grace"; rather, through the cross God says, "Confess your sin and I will shower you with mercy."

In all of this we are led finally to speak of the mystery of the cross. For we must confess that our understanding fails us. It is not that we lack intelligence or the capacity for clear thought. Rather, as H. R. Mackintosh so beautifully put it many years ago,

> the great reason why we fail to understand Calvary is not merely that we are not profound enough, it is that we are not good enough. It is because we are such strangers to sacrifice that God's sacrifice leaves us bewildered. It is because we love so little that his love is mysterious. We have never forgiven anybody at such a cost as his. We have never taken the initiative in putting a quarrel right with his kind of unreserved willingness to suffer. It is our unlikeness to God that hangs as an obscuring screen impeding our view, and we see the Atonement so often through the frosted glass of our own lovelessness.[28]

Thus, as Luther saw so clearly, "the cross puts everything to the test." It tests our complacent religion and finds it wanting. It tests our tidy doctrinal systems in which we take such pride and with which we confine God within the bounds of our own feeble understanding. The cross probes ever deeper into the lairs of our self-righteousness. It wounds. It strips away. It shatters. It lays bare.

But having wounded, stripped away, shattered, and laid bare, the cross heals, the cross binds up, the cross recreates. Through the cross God heals in ways that we could not have dreamed. God binds up to an extent that we could not have imagined. God recreates in ways that we could not have foreseen. God stirs newness and hope that are beyond telling. Through the cross God does "impossibilities."

And not only once does the cross put our lives to the test, but again and again. And yet again. The cross continues to call down the unruly self, so prone to swell and preen and to mistake the Spirit's gifts for its own solid accomplishments. And it continues to comfort and restore the fragile or wounded self, making it able and willing to take up Jesus' cross after him.

(3) *The way of the cross provides the model for God's new social order, the messianic community.* In proclaiming the Kingdom of God and in calling people to follow him, Jesus summoned people into a new kind of community, an alternative social order. At the very moment when his popularity seemed the

greatest, when the multitudes thronged about him, Jesus issued his first sharp words of warning: "If anyone comes to me and does not hate his own father and mother and wife and children and brothers and sisters, yes, and even his own life, he cannot be my disciple. Whoever does not bear his own cross and come after me, cannot be my disciple" (Lk. 14:26-27). His point was that in a society bound by powerful religious and family ties, his disciples must shake loose from such ties so that they can live the radically new kind of life to which he calls them.

Entering the Kingdom means nothing less than participating in an alternative order, one that stands in sharp and disturbing contrast to the dominant ways of thinking and acting. In Christ's new community people forgive as God has forgiven them (Mt. 6:12-14; 18:32). In this new community suffering servanthood replaces dominion or lordship over others. "The world's rulers," Jesus said, "lord it over their subjects, and their great men make them feel the weight of authority. That is not the way with you; among you, whoever wants to be great must be your servant . . . ." (Mk. 10:42-44; cf. Jn. 13:1-17).

In this new community of cross-bearing, forgiveness and peace absorbs hostility and abuse. In this community one learns to love freely and indiscriminately—a reflection of the way God loves. "But you must love your enemies, and do good and lend without expecting return; . . . you will be sons of the Most High, because he himself is kind to the ungrateful and the selfish. Be compassionate as your Father is compassionate" (Lk. 6:35-36; cf. Mt. 5:43-48).

In this new community people release their grip upon possessions and share freely with those in need (Mt. 6:25-33; Lk. 12:32-34). Here we learn to care for the people society has rejected, to receive the handicapped, the retarded, the poor, the prisoners—all of those whom Jesus called "the least of these" (Mt. 25:40). And in this new community people learn to endure the hostility of a world that cannot bear to have its *modus operandi* challenged. This new community, in short, follows the way that Jesus went—the way that led to the cross. It becomes a concrete, social expression of the way of the cross.

Through baptism in the name of Christ one experiences the radical new orientation that marks one as part of this new community. In baptism into Christ's death we die to the power of sin. In baptism we lay Christ's whole life story over the grid of our own life story. We are crucified with him. We are buried with him. We are raised with him. We live with him (Rom. 6:3-11).

In baptism we receive a new identity. We embrace a new guiding vision for our lives, a new story to tell and to live by. This new story is the story of Christ's dying and rising, and it becomes for us the lifelong story of our own repenting and being converted. In the drama of baptism one finds a new orientation to the world. Baptism symbolizes the obliteration of old distinctions, of old habits, of old racial and economic barriers. Through baptism one enters a community of equals, one where people have given up hope in themselves and the old securities. "Baptized into union with him," Paul writes, "you have all put on Christ as a garment. There is no such thing as Jew and Greek, slave and free man, male and female, for you are all one person in Christ Jesus" (Gal. 3:27-28). Paul uses the same baptismal language when he speaks of growth in Christ-like character: "then put on the garments that suit God's chosen people, his own, his beloved: compassion, kindness, humility, gentleness, patience. Be forbearing with one another, and forgiving where any of you have cause for complaint" (Col. 3:12-13).

In the powerful experience of baptism God sets us apart. We embrace a new story for our lives. Baptism is not simply the initiatory rite of Christian faith, a step on the way to salvation; rather it symbolizes the whole of that life, which is a constant dying and rising with Christ. In the faithful practice of baptism we proclaim to the world what kind of community we intend to be. We proclaim that God empowers us to be a cruciform people.

If baptism serves as the sign of our entry into the way of the cross, the Lord's supper serves as the sign of our journey along that way. In the weekly supper we renew our fellowship with the Crucified One. We remember his sufferings and meditate on what he wrought for us in the atonement. We experience his presence with us and hear again the call to share with him in his sufferings (Phil. 3:10-11; 1 Pet. 4:13).

Hounded constantly by the world's vision of success and power, we are confronted, around Christ's table, with a contrary vision—the way of weakness and the power of suffering love. Week by week that vision takes hold of us. Week by week, as we gather around the table, we are fashioned by God into a cruciform people. There we gradually find ourselves open to ways of living in this world that we had not considered possible.

The cross thus puts our churches to the test. It exposes our smug elitism, our affluent isolation. It strikes at the social and racial barriers we have inherited and so comfortably perpetuate. It shames us for our church fights, for our readiness to call it quits with our sisters and brothers. And when we lazily embrace the spirit of the age, becoming little more than "Christ clubs," the cross reawakens us to our first calling.

Christ continually points his followers to the way of the cross. I turn now to look further at the challenge of following this way in contemporary Western culture.

The Way of the Cross

To speak of following the way of the cross in Western culture today, we must first look at the dominant vision of the good life that has gradually descended upon the West since the age of Enlightenment. The Enlightenment has bequeathed our modern world many good things, but as we have seen in previous chapters, its blessings were mixed, its legacy deeply ironic. The Enlightenment values of progress and individualism, when combined with astounding technological virtuosity and economic prosperity, created a new dominant vision of the good life.

The Enlightenment philosopher David Hume (d. 1776) well described this vision, and his description could serve as a credo of the modern age:

> Fasting, penance, mortification, self denial, humility, silence, solitude, and the whole train of monkish virtues:—for what reason are they everywhere rejected by men of sense, but because they serve to no manner of purpose; neither advance a man's fortune in the world, nor render him a more valuable member of society;

neither qualify him for the entertainment of company, nor increase his power of self enjoyment? We observe, on the contrary, that they cross all these desirable ends; stupify the understanding and harden the heart, obscure the fancy and sour the temper.[29]

Hume here states in bald terms a basic assumption that has become a staple of the modern Western ethos. That assumption can be stated simply: the highest purpose of human life is happiness and well-being in this world, and everything that might detract from that happiness or compromise it must be avoided.

As secularization has progressed from Hume's eighteenth century to Hugh Hefner's twentieth century, that assumption has become ever more broadly accepted and deeply embedded. In the secular ethos of today the very idea that anyone would choose to follow the way of suffering has become nearly incomprehensible. Most of us, in our heart of hearts, view all suffering as bad. For most of us the highest good has become the removal of all suffering. We seek above all peace, safety, pleasure, the removal of all pain. As much as possible suffering is to be avoided. And so we marshall all the technology, wealth, and ingenuity at our disposal to do that.

Take a common argument, for instance. Today we commonly hear the argument that it is better for preborn or defective newborn children to die rather than experience a life of suffering or hardship. Such an argument, I must say, has always struck me as terribly odd. I realize that complex and difficult situations arise and that sometimes we must make tragic decisions. But the fact that so many people now find such sweeping arguments compelling only reflects the deep entrenchment of secular assumptions about suffering and the nature of the good life.[30]

Such assumptions about suffering naturally result from the radically individualistic worldview of our time. At the heart of this worldview lies stress on "rights," uninhibited free choice, and self-fulfillment. In such a worldview the "self-maximizer" replaces the "covenant-keeper," as Lewis Smedes has put it.[31]

A recent study by a California sociologist illumines this worldview in a striking way. Attempting to understand the deep tensions over the abortion issue, she conducted extensive interviews with a group of prolife activists and with a group of pro-abortion activists. She found that the two groups held two sharply divergent visions of the world.

The prolife activists as a whole were deeply religious. They believed in an overarching divine plan for human life. They viewed this present life as spiritual training for a life to come, and thus tended to accept the pain and disappointments that life brought as part of this training. They did not readily welcome suffering, but viewed it as an often necessary part of the moral life lived under God.

The pro-abortion worldview, in contrast, was "not centered around a Divine Being, but rather around a belief in the highest abilities of human beings." The pro-abortion activists were utilitarian and this-worldly, convinced that they must do all within their power to fulfill their lives in the here and now. To them suffering carried no ennobling or spiritual purpose. They viewed suffering, the researcher reported, "as stupid, as a waste, and as a failure, particularly when technology exists to eliminate it."[32] In their view life should be free of all unwanted burdens.

This assumption about suffering clearly dominates our culture. It holds powerful sway, even over those who would oppose the blatantly secular worldview of the pro-abortion activists. As William May put it, "This generation is oriented to itself with a vengeance. Abortion protects it at one end and a discard pile for the aged protects it from inconvenience at the other."[33]

In such an ethos Jesus' call to bear the cross after him becomes nearly incomprehensible. With this dominant vision of the good life, Paul's testimony to being "crucified with Christ" becomes almost nonsensical. Jesus' call to forsake everything, to "hate one's own life also" (Lk. 14:26), and his charge that he who would save his life must lose it (Mk. 8:35-36) simply do not make sense to people who live by this vision of the good life.

For the Christian faith to remain popular in such an ethos (as it has done), Jesus' call to follow the way of the cross must be significantly altered. The cross must, in Goethe's phrase, be "wreathed in roses." It must become a gentle, soothing symbol, stirring people toward fulfilling their potential, enlarging their security, and ensuring their added comforts. The ignominy of the cross must be overshadowed by the glory of the resurrection. The theology of the cross must give way to a theology of glory. Paul's words about the "scandal" of preaching Christ crucified (1 Cor. 1:23) must be "so overlaid with devotional wadding that we can no longer feel their aggressive thrust."[34] The cross, in short, must be displaced or at least redefined.

The early Corinthian church faced similar pressures. Apparently an influential group in the congregation believed that resurrection life had superseded life under the cross. They believed that the fullness of eternity was theirs already, that the Christian life was a life filled with glory, success, triumph, and bounty. They had little place for the cross or the hardships Paul faced. "Already you are filled!" (1 Cor. 4:8), Paul chided them.

We must see that these Christians, with their theology of glory, stood close to Paul himself in an important way. They had embraced one important strand of Paul's teaching but had left out another. Indeed, baptism entailed a rising with Christ (Rom. 6:4ff). Indeed, conversion brought a higher wisdom from God (1 Cor. 1:20-31). Indeed, "Christ Jesus abolished death and brought life and immortality to light through the gospel" (2 Tim. 1:10). But though the Corinthian Christians understood the power of the resurrection, they misunderstood the place of the cross. Paul therefore counters with a sharp corrective. He says that though Christians have been raised with Christ they still live in the body with all its humbling limitations (1 Cor. 4:8-13). He stresses that Christ alone has been raised in glory thus far—the Christian's resurrection to glory remains in the future. The new age has indeed broken into the old one, but it has not yet been consummated so Christians must wait with longing and patience.

Christ thus remains for them the Crucified One. Christian discipleship takes its shape from the cross. So Paul encourages the Corinthians to abandon their exalted "balcony" attitude toward the world and to come down into the arena. He calls them from the "other-worldly" glories of the resurrection to the "this-worldly" demands of bearing the cross in the here and now. He encourages them to exchange their "wisdom," "strength," and "respectability" for the weak, despised, and vulnerable position of the apostles. In this way the Corinthian Christians may be drawn more fully into the self-renouncing process (1 Cor. 4:9-13; cf. 2 Cor. 4:2-10).[35]

For us, as for the Corinthian Christians, the pattern of cross and resurrection remains the pattern for Christian existence in this world. We bear the cross having experienced the aura of the resurrection. The resurrection does not eclipse the cross in this earthly life, but it does cast the cross in a very different light. In the godforsakenness of his cross, Christ drew out the sting of despair and hopelessness from human life so that all those who bear the cross after him might see it in light of God's final victory. Thus Ernst Käsemann could remark that the "glory of Jesus consists in the fact that he makes his disciples on earth willing and capable to bear the cross after him."[36]

In his devotional classic, *A Testament of Devotion*, Thomas Kelly beautifully captures God's call into the way of the cross:

> The cross as dogma is painless speculation; the cross as lived suffering is anguish and glory. Yet God, out of the pattern of his own heart, has planted the cross along the road of holy obedience. And He enacts in the hearts of those He loves the miracle of willingness to welcome suffering and to know it for what it is—the final seal of His gracious love. I dare not urge you to your cross. But He, more powerfully, speaks within you and me, to our truest selves, in our truest moments, and disquiets us with the world's needs. By inner persuasion He draws us to a few very definite tasks, our tasks, God's burdened heart particularizing His burdens in us.[37]

Following the way of the cross today, in a culture where such a way scarcely makes any sense at all, will mean creating a kind of separatist community. It will mean living in a different ethos, one where the call to bear the cross becomes intelligible, a community that provides models of what following that way will look like. It will mean, as we will see further in the next chapter, intentionally nurturing a community standing in sharp contrast to the dominant secular ethos of our time.

Notes

Epigraphs: Martin Luther; Morris A. Eames, *The Philosophy of Alexander Campbell* (Bethany, W.V.: Bethany College, 1966), p. 84.

[1]Barton W. Stone, *Atonement, The Substance of Two Letters Written to a Friend* (Lexington, Ky., 1805). For the background and setting of this work, see D. Newell Williams, "The Theology of the Great Revival in the West as Seen Through the Life and Thought of Barton W. Stone" (Ph.D. diss., Vanderbilt University, 1979), pp. 96-107.

[2]Alexander Campbell, *The Christian System* (1835; reprint ed., Nashville, Tenn.: Gospel Advocate, 1970), pp. 26, 23. Campbell states his agreement with Luther that the doctrine of justification provides the real test of a church's standing or falling (p. 153).

[3]Ibid., pp. 22-25.

[4]The exchange began with Barton Stone, "Atonement," *Millennial Harbinger* 4, 2nd series (June 1840):243-46, and Alexander Campbell, "A. C.'s Reply to Barton Stone," ibid., pp. 246-50 [also in *Christian Messenger* 11 (September 1840):3-28]. See especially their later exchange in "Atonement—No. IV," ibid., pp. 464-73.

[5]Alexander Campbell, "Sermons to Young Preachers—No. 4," *Christian Baptist* 7 (April 5, 1830):213-215. I am indebted to Bill Love for this reference.

[6]See for example, Jesse L. Sewell, "The Bible," in David Lipscomb, *Life and Sermons of Jesse L. Sewell* (Nashville, Tenn.: McQuiddy, 1891), pp. 128-29; T. W. Brents, *The Gospel Plan of Salvation*, 13th ed. (Nashville, Tenn.: Gospel Advocate, 1950), pp. 160-62; and James D. Bales, *The Hub of the Bible, or Acts Two Analyzed* (Rosemead, Calif.: Old Paths, 1960), p. 4.

[7]John Sweeney, *Sweeney's Sermons* (Nashville, Tenn.: Gospel Advocate, 1892), pp. 252-53.

[8]See for example, Jesse L. Sewell, "What Must I Do to be Saved?" in *Life and Sermons*, pp. 150-63, and N. B. Hardeman, "What Must I Do to be Saved?" in *Tabernacle Sermons* (Nashville, Tenn.: McQuiddy, 1922), pp. 176-85.

[9]Brents, *Gospel Plan of Salvation*, 13th ed. (1950). In Brent's widely

read collection of sermons entitled *Gospel Sermons* (Nashville, Tenn.: McQuiddy, 1918), nine out of twenty-one sermons make some mention of the death of Christ.

[10]Bill Love, *The Crux of the Matter: A Comparison of New Testament and Restoration Preaching* (manuscript in progress). I am indebted to Bill Love for sharing some of his research with me and for giving me permission to use it.

[11]C. L. Loos, "The Cross," *Millennial Harbinger* 40 (1869):604-607. Loos, however, reflects a common misunderstanding when he says that "we know God does not suffer, that he cannot suffer."

[12]On the nature of God's "covenant" and "covenant love" (*hesed*) in the Old Testament, see John L. McKenzie, "Aspects of Old Testament Thought," in *Jerome Biblical Commentary* (Englewood Cliffs, N.J.: Prentice-Hall, 1968), 2:749-53, and Bernhard W. Anderson, "The Biblical Ethic of Obedience," *Christian Scholar* 39 (March 1956):66-71. For a different perspective, see also William F. May, "Code, Covenant, Contract, or Philanthropy," *Hastings Center Report* 5 (December 1975):29-38.

[13]K. C. Moser, *The Way of Salvation* (Nashville, Tenn., 1932; reprint ed., Delight, Ark.: Gospel Light, 1933), pp. 117-118, 122, 123.

[14]Richard T. Hughes, "Are Restorationists Evangelicals?" in *Varieties of American Evangelicalism*, ed. Donald Dayton and Robert Johnston (Knoxville, Tenn.: University of Tennessee, 1990).

[15]G. C. Brewer, "Read This Book," *Gospel Advocate* 75 (May 11, 1933):434. Brewer said that Moser's book was "one of the best little books that came from any press in 1932."

[16]Brewer, "Grace and Salvation," *Abilene Christian College Bible Lectures, 1952* (Austin, Tex.: Firm Foundation, 1952), p. 115. See also Brewer, "Christ Today, Our Mediator and High Priest," ibid. (1938), p. 208. Regarding Brewer's influence, J. D. Tant remarked in 1934 that "no man in the brotherhood stands higher and has the confidence of the entire church above Brewer." *Firm Foundation* 51 (June 12, 1934):5.

[17]See H. Wheeler Robinson, "The Cross of the Servant," in *The Cross in the Old Testament* (London, Eng.: SCM, 1955), pp. 59-114, and Walter Zimmerli and Joachim Jeremias, *The Servant of God* (Naperville, Ill.: Alec R. Allenson, 1957).

[18]Love, *Crux of the Matter*.

[19]See Hendrikus Berkhof, *Christ and the Powers*, trans. John H. Yoder (Scottdale, Pa.: Herald, 1962); G. B. Caird, *Principalities and Powers: A Study in Pauline Theology* (Oxford, Eng.: Clarendon, 1956); and G. H. C. MacGregor, "Principalities and Powers: The Cosmic Background of Paul's Thought," *New Testament Studies 1* (1954): 17-28.

[20]See Robert J. Daly, *The Origins of the Christian Doctrine of Sacrifice* (Philadelphia, Pa.: Fortress, 1978), and James D. G. Dunn, "Paul's Understanding of the Death of Jesus as Sacrifice," in *Sacrifice and Redemption*, ed. S. W. Sykes (Cambridge, Eng.: Cambridge University, 1989).

[21]On this imagery see I. Howard Marshall, "The Development of the Concept of Redemption in the New Testament," in *Reconciliation and Hope*, ed. Robert Banks (Grand Rapids, Mich.: Eerdmans, 1974), pp. 153-69.

[22]See John Driver, *Understanding the Atonement for the Mission of the Church* (Scottdale, Pa.: Herald, 1988), pp. 177-86, 213-29.

[23]Ibid., p. 191.

[24]See Joachim Jeremias, "Justification by Faith," in *The Central Message of the New Testament* (New York: Scribner's, 1965), pp. 51-70; Markus Barth, *Justification: Pauline Texts Interpreted in the Light of the Old and New Testaments*, trans. A. M. Woodruf (Grand Rapids, Mich.: Eerdmans, 1971); and Luke T. Johnson, "Romans 3:21-26 and the Faith of Jesus," *Catholic Biblical Quarterly* 44 (1982):77-90.

[25]C. A. Dismore, *Atonement in Literature and Life* (1906), quoted in J. K. Mozley, *The Impassibility of God: A Survey of Christian Thought* (Cambridge, Eng.: Cambridge University, 1926), p. 148.

[26]Stanley Hauerwas, *Vision and Virtue* (Notre Dame, Ind.: University of Notre Dame, 1974), p. 192.

[27]Hauerwas, "Self Deception and Autobiography: Reflections on Speer's *Inside the Third Reich*," in *Truthfulness and Tragedy* (Notre Dame, Ind.: University of Notre Dame, 1977), p. 98. See also David Myers, *The Inflated Self: Human Illusions and the Call to Hope* (New York: Seabury, 1980), esp. pp. 45-81.

[28]H. R. Mackintosh, *Sermons* (New York: Scribner's, 1938), p. 177. Cf. Mackintosh, *The Christian Experience of Forgiveness* (New York: Harper, 1927), pp. 179-87, 229-31.

[29]David Hume, *Enquiry Into Morals*, ed. L. A. Selby-Bigge (Oxford, Eng.: Oxford University, 1957), p. 270.

[30]See Stanley Hauerwas, *Suffering Presence* (Notre Dame, Ind.: University of Notre Dame, 1986), pp. 23-38.

[31]Lewis Smedes, *Mere Morality: What God Expects from Ordinary People* (Grand Rapids, Mich.: Eerdmans, 1983), p. 160.

[32]Kristin Luker, *Abortion and the Politics of Motherhood* (Berkeley, Calif.: University of California, 1984), pp. 158-191.

[33]William F. May, "The Metaphysical Plight of the Family," *Hastings Center Studies* 2 (1974):29.

[34]Ernst Käsemann, "The Pauline Theology of the Cross," *Interpretation* 24 (April 1970):156.

[35]On the key passages where Paul develops this paradox of the cross (1 Cor. 4:9-13; 2 Cor. 4:7-15; 6:1-10), see Anthony T. Hanson, *The Paradox of the Cross in the Thought of St. Paul* (Sheffield, Eng.: Journal for the Study of the Old Testament, 1988), pp. 5-78.

[36]Käsemann, "Theology of the Cross," p. 177.

[37]Thomas Kelly, *A Testament of Devotion* (New York: Harper & Brothers, 1944), pp. 71-72.

6

The Holy Spirit and the Spirit of the Age

O God's own people, O Body of Christ, O highborn race of foreigners on earth, you do not belong here, you belong somewhere else. . . . [Therefore] let longing for the everlasting Jerusalem grow and be strengthened in your hearts.
—*Augustine of Hippo (416)*

The church today is so notoriously like a clearance sale in all sorts of religious goods that we can no longer afford to identify Jesus with Christendom.
—*Ernst Käsemann (1970)*

Being a cruciform church, as we have seen, means following the way of self-renouncement. It means participating in the cross as a scandalous event. Though we easily avoid this scandal, it is precisely here that the cross takes us. It compels us to find a distinct identity in relation to a world that finds the cruciform life unimaginable and even repugnant.

Looking to Our Past

Our identity as a movement takes shape as we wrestle with the tension between the church and the world, or more precisely, the tension between a sense of being arrayed against the world and a sense of being comfortably at home in it.

Put in sociological terms, we can view this tension as between "sect" and "church" (or "denomination"). Ernst Troeltsch made the classic distinction:

> The Church is an institution which has been endowed with grace and salvation as the result of the work of Redemption; it is able to receive the masses, and to adjust itself to the world, because, to a certain extent, it can afford to ignore the need for subjective holiness for the sake of the objective treasures of grace and of redemption.
>
> The sect is a voluntary society, composed of strict and definite Christian believers bound to each other by the fact that all have experienced the "new Birth." These believers live apart from the world, are limited to small groups, and in varying degrees within their own circle set up the Christian order based on love; all this is done in preparation for and expectation of the coming kingdom of God.[1]

The features of the "sect" have characterized in varying degrees the historic stream of "free churches" or "believers' churches" that emerged as one branch of the sixteenth-century Protestant Reformation. Empowered by their dissent against the state churches filled with hordes of nominally converted people, the Believers' Churches were marked by "earnestness, witness, covenant (signing their names), discipline, mutual aid, [and a] simple pattern of worship."[2] Among the four historic marks of the church (unity, holiness, catholicity, and apostolicity), these churches stressed the central place of holiness. Through the experience of spiritual rebirth and the rigorous exercise of discipline in their ranks they sought to keep the church pure and unblemished by the world.

The terms "gathered church" and "visible sainthood" emerged to express this ideal. Supporting this emphasis, in most cases, was a dark view of the fall of the church and the necessity for restoration of apostolic purity. Speaking of the early Anabaptists, one scholar wrote that "they wished to restore the early church at Jerusalem as a community of saints sharply separated from the world."[3]

Because of this dissenting stance and spiritual rigor, the officially established churches often viewed Christians of the Believers' Churches as troublers of Zion, as moralists, fanatics, "enthusiasts," and schismatics. And indeed, as George Williams wryly noted, the Believers' Churches often have been "leavers' churches."[4] Furthermore, such dissenters have tended to let their stress on moral and doctrinal purity produce a works righteousness, thus overshadowing the centrality of grace.

But despite the theological pitfalls to which they are subject, the Believers' Churches have held up a powerful witness to the church as a "communion of saints" arrayed against the "world, the flesh, and the devil." They have been able to generate great energy, commitment, and sacrifice. And they have provided, time and again, the sharp and prophetic voices that have stirred renewal among the comfortable and the uncommitted.

The churches of the early Stone-Campbell movement stood squarely in this tradition. In fact, with the disestablishment of religion and the rise of voluntarism, American Protestantism as a whole was shaped profoundly by the "free church" ideal. This influence was most pronounced among the groups that competed for souls along the westward-moving frontier—especially the Baptists, Methodists, and "Christians." In the flames of revivalism new communities of believers were forged and the dross of worldliness was drawn off by strict discipline. The simple, unadorned, unpretentious piety of primitive Christianity captured their imaginations, and out of that vision they sought to live in bold contrast to the world.

Nowhere is this vision clearer among the Stoneite "Christians" than in the life of Joseph Thomas, the "White Pilgrim." Upon his immersion in 1811 Thomas gradually grew convinced that division in the church had resulted from pride, self-interest, and the fashions of the world; he realized, therefore, that he must reject such fashions and adopt a primitive simplicity in his lifestyle. By 1815 Thomas had sold his farm and possessions and "put off my fashionable clothing." As a result he felt free "from the encumbrances and attachments of the world" and thus ready to preach the gospel in the ancient way. He donned a white robe and for the rest of his life preached the gospel throughout the Blue Ridge region.

Today we may view the Pilgrim as quaint, eccentric, or even laughable. But his example points us to the heart of the restoration ideal among the early "Christians" of the Stone movement. Their chief protest, Richard Hughes concludes, was "against a Christianity encumbered by the cares and fashions of this world. They were committed instead to a faith wherein the Saints would minister to the poor and the downtrodden and would wash one another's feet as a sign of the humility that befitted followers of the Lamb."[5] Their sectarian stance was based, not on a carefully demarcated doctrinal platform, but rather on a powerful vision of the holy and separate life to which believers are called. (The doctrinal sectarianism, however, would come in due time.)

In the opening years of the nineteenth century this powerful vision of the separate and holy life was sustained by millennial expectations. Centuries of "human invention" had dammed up the streams of godliness and vital piety. But now, many believed, the dam was cracking and the pure waters beginning to flow again. What motivated them and what bound them together were not church structures, offices, and rules but rather the rushing sound of the approaching millennium. The old order, dominated by creeds, rules, and the clergy, was passing away. The new was approaching.

As long as this millennial fervor remained kindled there was little interest in or attention to the formal strictures of church discipline. For in such an atmosphere the spirit of separation from the world flourished on its own. For a time this spirit combined with a stirring display of unity among diverse believers. Many believed that nothing less than a restoration of pure apostolic Christianity was occurring. The old, time-worn boundaries between believers would fall away forever; they would be replaced by a compelling vision of Christ-like holiness which would draw all believers into one great communion. A dazzling display of Christian unity would explode in America and around the world. The themes of restoration, holiness, and unity all intertwined as these early pioneers of our movement attempted to describe their expectations.

But by the 1830s and 1840s the revival fires had cooled. The original millennial vision was beginning to dim. It became increasingly clear that religious pluralism in America would not vanish under the sway of the "ancient gospel." The time-worn boundaries would not fall away. A grand and glorious unity would not transpire.

The Stone-Campbell movement thus began to take shape as a separate religious group. Leaders began attending to the organizational and structural needs that attend such groups. They grew increasingly preoccupied with maintaining institutional momentum and with defending their boundaries.

At the same time the great zeal for holiness and for separation from the world waned in the movement. In 1843 Alexander Campbell wrote that one of the greatest needs among the churches was "much less conformity to the world—its idle pomp and pageantry—its frivolous amusements—its selfishness and covetousness—its pride and vanity." What was needed, he said, was "a more exemplary separation from the spirit and fashion of the world." In the decades that followed many of the movement's most respected leaders lamented that "one by one the bad habits of a fashionable Christianity are creeping in upon us."[6]

With the cooling of the original vision, church discipline became more and more an issue of study and debate as the churches took upon themselves the task of enforcing what they perceived as the moral standards of the New Testament. In the period before 1865, church records show that disfellowshipping was practiced fairly widely and for a number of reasons. Members were disciplined for participation in "worldly allurements" such as dancing, "games of chance," and "profane swearing"; for drunkenness; for marrying "unbelievers" (which on occasion meant those outside the movement); for divorce; for economic misconduct; and for a few other offenses.

Offenses related to money seem particularly common, a judgment supported by Alexander Campbell's comment in 1844: "Many of the controversies and cases of discipline which occur in churches, arise from this foredoomed and soulwithering passion for wealth." On another occasion, when Campbell was asked about what to do with a member who drank and sold alcoholic beverages, he replied: "If, on remonstrance and admonition, he does not reform, put him away from the church."[7]

The excluding of offending members was fairly common among the churches before 1865. But by the end of the nineteenth century many of the churches in the movement had ceased such practice. The very notion of "withdrawing fellowship" was attacked and rejected by some church leaders. Behind this shift in practice lay a steady trend toward acculturation, toward a comfortable adaptation to the mores of middle-class urban society.[8] In sociological terms we can say that many churches moved steadily into denominational status.

During this period Churches of Christ, for the most part, vigorously resisted such trends. The members tended to be less affluent, less educated, more humble in the eyes of the world. They were more a part of the rural, agrarian world of the South than the swelling urban centers of the North and East. In sociological terms they remained a sect.

Perhaps the most influential voice among Churches of Christ in that period was that of David Lipscomb. Catching the spirit of Lipscomb's life, one of his contemporaries noted that he "lives in utter disregard of the notions of the world." In a characteristic passage, Lipscomb wrote that the "religion of Christ was not only adapted to the common people, but despite all theories to the contrary, they are those best fitted to maintain and spread that religion. The rich corrupt it, the rich pervert it to suit their own fashionable ways."[9] God's people, he believed, rejected worldly fashion and sought simplicity. For this reason he was appalled in 1892 when he heard that an Atlanta church had spent $30,000 on its new building.

But, if in the nineteenth century Churches of Christ largely resisted the acculturation that appeared in many Disciples churches, by the early decades of the twentieth century they began to face similar tensions.

Consider an episode in the 1920s. In 1922 a young preacher named John Allen Hudson came to work for a congregation in Memphis, Tennessee. His objective, he later wrote, was "the building of a commodious house of worship adequate to every need." He threw himself to the task of raising money, and he was quite successful. As a result, the congregation was able to purchase a lot on Union Avenue; then in 1925 "our beautiful new church home" was completed. In a lengthy report to the *Gospel Advocate*, Hudson estimated its value at $125,000— an enormous sum for a time when one could buy a new Ford for something over $300.[10]

Hudson's published report was followed by a sharp and lengthy response from James A. Allen, editor of the *Advocate*. "Brother Hudson's account of his labors," Allen first noted, "shows the rapid and dangerous progress that many of our preachers are making back to the habits of the professional 'pastor.'" But then, with great feeling, he spoke to his major concern:

> A meetinghouse that has one hundred and twenty-five thousand dollars tied up in it is a satire on the spirit and genius of Christianity. Such a thing is a sin that cries to heaven and will continue to so cry until it is sold and that huge amount of money given to the poor or used to have the gospel preached to those who are lost.

"Such a house and such surroundings," he continued, "breed a spirit of worldliness that is incompatible with the true worship and service of God." In fact, "anything that is incompatible with humility, spirituality, and poverty of spirit is out of place."

In a paragraph that could just as well have been written by his predecessor David Lipscomb, Allen distilled his protest:

> Jesus was born in a stable. He selected to be his apostles men who were penniless. In the age when the church grew most rapidly most of its members were common laboring people; and while some few of its members were men of wealth, they were taught to preserve their wealth by giving it away. They were taught to give to two objects—to help the poor and to have the gospel preached. Money is dissipated, thrown away, when given to the thousand and one fads and fancies suggested by the professional promoters.[11]

In this episode we see a basic clash of attitudes and values regarding human culture. John Allen Hudson and James A. Allen both agreed on the "plan of salvation," the appropriate "acts of worship," and other doctrinal matters that distinguished Churches of Christ. But they held radically different views of the church's priorities and role in culture. In this they reflect the growing tensions between rural and urban values.

It takes no special insight to see that by the 1960s Churches of Christ, for the most part, had taken their stand with the John Allen Hudsons rather than the David Lipscombs and James A. Allens. What may be harder to see is just how much they had changed to get there.

Against the World for the World

As this glimpse into our past indicates, the relationship of Churches of Christ to their surrounding culture has been fraught with tensions and ironies. We do not have to look far in our own history to confront again the age-old paradoxical question, "How can the church be *in* the world but not *of* the world?" To put the dilemma differently, how can we detach ourselves from worldly values, yet at the same time serve the world in compassionate and sacrificial ways? How, in short, should the church relate to its surrounding culture today?

H. Richard Niebuhr, in his famous book *Christ and Culture*, developed a helpful model of the various ways Christians through the ages have attempted to relate their faith to the surrounding culture.[12] Niebuhr distinguished five types:

(1) *Christ against culture.* In this view people of faith should seek to separate themselves from the prevailing culture. They must stand apart from the generally accepted behavior patterns, institutions, and modes of thought. The church must become a "withdrawn community," for the dominant culture is always fallen, held under the sway of the "powers" and largely beyond redemption.

(2) *Christ of culture.* At the other extreme in Niebuhr's model are those who see a fundamental agreement between Christian faith and the highest values of the culture. In this view "Jesus often appears as a great hero of human cultural history; ... In Him, it is believed, the aspirations of men toward their values are brought to a point of culmination." This perspective minimizes any significant differences between the way of Christ

and the way of the world. The highest aspirations and ideals of the culture are viewed as basically Christian.

Between these two extreme positions Niebuhr saw three mediating positions. All three of these positions acknowledge a fundamental tension between Christian faith and culture, but all three attempt to relate them in some meaningful way. All stress that simple withdrawal from society is not the appropriate response.

(3) *Christ above culture.* This approach attempts to synthesize eternal values with cultural values. It appreciates the values and aspirations of the prevailing culture, but proclaims that only Christ can fulfill such aspirations. Thus "Christ enters into life from above with gifts which human aspiration has not envisioned and which human effort cannot attain unless he relates men to a supernatural society and a new value-center." A gulf remains fixed between Christ and culture. The stringent demands of Christ cannot be fitted snugly with the ideals for human life held up by society. But because God is Creator and Lord of the world, culture cannot finally be opposed to Christ. Thus the highest cultural aspirations point to and find their completion in Christ.

(4) *Christ and culture in paradox.* Advocates of this perspective agree with the Christ-against-culture advocates that the values of God's kingdom differ sharply from the values of the world. They agree that "the whole edifice of culture is cracked and madly askew," that it is "godless and sick unto death." Yet, unlike those who advocate withdrawal from the culture, advocates of this perspective acknowledge that culture in unavoidable. They believe that Christians must live in the world even though it is corrupt. Christians must face the perpetual tension of fulfilling their obligations in both realms. In this tension, they believe, compromise frequently occurs. Evil easily taints one. Christians thus live precariously in this tension, always trusting God's mercy and forgiveness.

(5) *Christ the transformer of culture.* As with three of the four other views, this one recognizes that corruption permeates human culture. But unlike the other views, it adopts a more positive and hopeful stance toward culture. It emphasizes God as Creator. Through the redemptive work of Christ, God not

only reconciles the sinner but also renews the created order. Thus advocates of this view believe that any area of culture can be transformed by Christ. Some even hold out the possibility of universal cultural renewal in this world. Thus all of human culture becomes "subject to the great conversion that ensues when God makes a new beginning for man."

With these five types Niebuhr attempted to set forth the basic options Christians throughout history have taken in relating their faith to the larger culture. At one extreme is withdrawal from culture, at the other wide embrace of culture. In between are three positions all attempting to mediate between Christ and culture. Niebuhr did not claim that any one of these five comprises *the* Christian answer. All reflect certain biblical themes. All have certain strengths to commend them. But Niebuhr himself clearly favors the transformational stance, for it is the only one of the five against which he lodges no criticisms at all.

Niebuhr's typology serves us well as we wrestle with the thorny problem of the church's relationship to the world. It properly focuses on the church's necessary interaction with the world. It highlights the challenge of being *in* the world but not *of* the world. But as John Howard Yoder and others have argued, Niebuhr subtly rigged his typology so that the transformational model he himself favored emerges as the clear solution to the problem. In other words, he sets up the problem as if the only real alternatives for the Christian are to take responsibility for the culture or to withdraw irresponsibly from it (or some variation on the two).[13]

Yoder calls this a Constantinian formulation of the problem. He argues that such a way of putting the issue presupposes the joining of church and world that occurred during the third and fourth centuries (symbolized by Emperor Constantine's conversion to Christianity). In the Constantinian situation the makeup of the church changed dramatically. Up to that time Christians were a minority in the empire. They faced regular opposition and sporadic persecution. Being a Christian required courage and firm commitment.

But after the Christian faith became officially sanctioned, and its profession a badge of respectability, almost everyone became a church member. Being a Christian required little courage, commitment, or sacrifice. Christianity took on majority status. With this new status church and world were fused in significant ways. The church began to view itself as responsible for christianizing the social order, for bringing all the institutions of society under the Christian umbrella. But the result was not the christianization of society. The result was the widespread dilution of Christ's high calling in the church.

Thus Yoder argues that Niebuhr's typology, despite its effectiveness as a tool of understanding, still retains the basic Constantinian assumption that the church must take responsibility for transforming the world into the Kingdom of God. In this view calls for Christians to withdraw or separate themselves from the culture are usually taken as signs of irresponsibility. Such a formulation of the problem, Yoder argues, misconstrues the biblical understanding of both the church and the world.[14]

To focus this issue we must look more closely at the biblical understanding. In the New Testament "world" can refer to the universe as a whole or to planet earth and its inhabitants (e.g. Rom. 1:8; Acts 17:24). But it is used most commonly, not in reference to a physical place, but to a system of values or a social order opposed to God.

The admonition in 1 John 2:15-16 puts its sharply: "Do not love the world, or the things in the world. When one loves the world, love for the Father is not in him. For all that is in the world, the lust of the flesh and the lust of the eyes and the pride of life, is not of the Father but is of the world."

Here the "world" is the realm of enmity with God. It is "the sum of the divine creation which has been shattered by the fall, which stands under the judgment of God, and in which Jesus Christ appears as redeemer." It is human society as it falls under the sway of the "lust of the flesh, the lust of the eyes, and the pride of life"—or as C. H. Dodd rendered these phrases, society "with its sensuality, [its] superficiality and pretentiousness, its materialism and its egoism."[15]

Thus the "world" is not primarily a place or material realm. It is not equivalent to created nature or to all human culture. Rather the "world" is the realm of unbelief, all of God's creation that has not yet come under God's dominion. It appears in and through all human culture. It manifests itself in everyone—including Christians—who choose not to profess Christ's lordship and make his way their way. The primary feature of this "world," as we saw in chapter four, is idolatry—the misplacing of our allegiances so that what is only finite and relative becomes ultimate and absolute.

In New Testament perspective, two realms (or aeons) exist side by side in human history. One is the world of sin and death, the other is the new humanity which makes up the body of Christ. Each of these two realms manifests itself socially or culturally. The old realm or "world" shows itself in the structures of human society in general (with its materialism, sensuality, racial barriers, economic conflicts, and constant declarations of human autonomy). The new realm (or aeon) shows itself in the church and the new social order it creates.

This new order (now becoming visible in the church) must be kept uncontaminated by the old (the "world"). It must maintain a distinctive quality of existence. It must uphold radically different values, treat people in radically different ways, and nurture within its community a different view of reality. As we saw in the last chapter, it must maintain an ethos where following the way of the cross becomes intelligible.

This means that the church must remain in a significant sense a withdrawn community. It must live in opposition to the "world." When we say that, however, we must speak carefully. Paul does not instruct the church to close itself off from the secular world (which would, in any case, be impossible) or to cease all association with the immoral people of the world (1 Cor. 5:9-10). There must be separation, to be sure, "but not of the usual kind. The church is not prohibited from entering the world; the world is excluded from entering the church."[16]

We are tempted to think that we can be God's holy and separate people by shutting ourselves off from the world or isolating ourselves from it. But it is never that simple. For the "world" is both without us and within us. Its boundary line runs through every human heart. For this reason, as James Cone said commenting on Israel's exodus from Egypt, it is far more difficult to get Egypt out of the people than the people out of Egypt.

The church thus does not simply withdraw from the "world." But it does stand apart from the "world" as a distinct entity. Rejecting the Constantinian assumption of Christianity's majority status, we must assume that the faithful Christian community will always occupy a minority status in its culture—even in a so-called "Christian" culture. This separate, minority status does not mean isolating oneself from society or failing to care for it. It does not mean self-righteously elevating oneself above other sinful human beings.

To the contrary, this sharp disavowal of the "world" and its values is done for the sake of the "world," for the love of the "world." We form a separate, distinctive community not to isolate and protect ourselves but because we believe that we can best serve the "world" by being the church.

By becoming a distinctive and set-apart community, the church serves the world in at least two important ways.

First, in taking its stance against the world, the church enables the world to see its true plight or lostness. As the realm of estrangement from God, the world lives by a clouded and distorted vision of reality. For this reason the world does not know that it is the world. It cannot recognize itself. It cannot name its most basic problem—rebellion against God and declaration of its own autonomy. In the language of John, it lives in darkness. Thus, as Stanley Hauerwas has written, "the church serves the world by giving the world the means to see itself truthfully."[17]

The church's first and highest calling, therefore, is to be the church. It shuns violence and retaliation, and thus helps the world see the way of peace. It eschews control and manipulation of people, and thus shows the world the way of respect and equality. It breaks down racial and social distinctions in its midst, and thus shows the world the sinfulness and injustice of its divisions between people. It lets go of its possessions with joy and gladness, and thus exposes the world's idolatrous attachment to its money and possessions.

The church thus serves as the "light of the world." Through its light the church summons all people to the praise of God. As a sixteenth-century Anabaptist writer put it, the church serves the world as a "lantern of righteousness." In the church, he said, "the light of grace is borne and held before the whole world, that its darkness, unbelief and blindness be thereby seen and made light, and that one may also learn to see and know the way of life."[18]

In this way at least part of the world may be able to recognize itself as "world." Part of the world may be able to see its lostness, its deception and chaos. At the same time, however, much of the world will scorn the church for attempting to show the world its true nature.

Second, in taking its stance against the world, the church creates an environment (or ethos) where people can develop the skills and virtues necessary to serve the world in sacrificial ways. The world, because it is the realm of estrangement from God, the realm of self-seeking and autonomy, does not (and indeed, cannot) provide the training ground where people learn to follow the way of the cross. Around us today we see an immense confusion concerning the proper way to live. As we have seen repeatedly in this book, the spirit of our age is marked by a relentless assertion of the self, a swelling contempt for self-restraint. The spirit of the age is the spirit of aggressive individualism.

Individualism invariably creates an atmosphere where people view themselves in competition with others for the good things that life offers. Thus one must assert oneself to make sure that one gets and keeps the good things of life, and that one gets and keeps more of them than others. Prophets of individualism rise up, promising people that they can "have it all" through bold self-assertion.

Such a world, of course, has its codes of ethics, its standards of social decorum, and it admonitions to service and goodwill. Such counsels do indeed check unrestrained self-assertion and elicit a measure of goodwill. And for that we should be thankful.

But in the final analysis the world's ethical counsels almost invariably hark back to self-interest and personal advancement. They inevitably tie regard for others to one's own egocentric gratification. So (the advice usually runs), if the narrow fixation on self fails to make one happy, then one should seek to find happiness by serving others. Or as one psychologist put it, "The task . . . is to train persons to act for the benefits of another because it is in their own self-interest."[19]

Such advice is about the best the world has to offer. Such training is about the best it can provide.

If we are to gain the skills and virtues required to follow the way of the cross, we will have to acquire them in a very different training ground. We will require a community that stands in sharp contrast to the dominant social order. For Jesus' way calls for kinds of caring that in the eyes of the world seem reckless and ill-advised. It calls for kinds of loving concern that seem beyond the reasonable call of duty.

Jesus' way calls, in short, for character traits and moral skills that appear either incomprehensible, foolish, or impossible to a world schooled only in the ethic of self-advancement. And indeed, Christians acknowledge that such traits and skills are impossible without the transforming power of the Holy Spirit that works in and through the body of Christ. Indeed, we acknowledge that the church can be the church only through the power of the Spirit.

The Church in the Power of the Spirit

In the New Testament, and especially in Paul, the Holy Spirit is the power of the messianic age that has dawned in Jesus Christ. The Spirit makes the crucified and resurrected Christ present in his body, the church. The Spirit extends Christ's lordship, and arms God's people in their battle against the "world," the "flesh," and the "powers." The Spirit moves us through enemy territory toward God's final victory, along the way offering us a quickening foretaste of the glory to come.

But far from leading us out of the world into other-worldly glories, far from spiriting us away from struggles in the worldly arena, the Spirit always directs us to the Crucified One and thus into the way of the cross. The Spirit forms in us the character traits required to follow that way. The Spirit implants in our hearts the strength to follow the way of weakness, the power to receive and care for the powerless, the peace to endure and absorb hostility.

In the doctrinal tradition of Churches of Christ we have not focused on the Spirit in this way. The intense debates in our heritage on the work of the Spirit have focused almost entirely on the Spirit's relation to the individual believer, on the indwelling Spirit as a private possession.[20] In this focus Churches of Christ reflect the powerful strain of individualism that runs through American culture and that has deeply influenced much of American Protestantism.

In the New Testament, however, emphasis falls not so much on the Spirit in the individual but on the Spirit dwelling and working in the midst of the two or three. Certainly individual believers possess the Spirit. As Paul put it, "If the Spirit of him who raised Jesus from the dead dwells in you, he who raised Christ Jesus from the dead will give life to your mortal bodies also through his Spirit which dwells in you" (Rom. 8:11; cf. 1 Cor. 3:16-17, 1 Thess. 4:8).

But life in the Spirit refers primarily to a new corporate reality. Life in the Spirit is life "in Christ," which means that one becomes part of a new community, a new humanity, one marked by the presence of the Spirit of God. "In Christ" there is a new corporate personality—Christians are united with Christ and with one another.

Paul speaks of this new corporate personality as the "body of Christ" (1 Cor. 12:12-27; Rom. 12:4-5). This body has many diverse members. But it is not simply a loose aggregate of believing individuals. Rather, it consists of mutually interdependent members, drawn by the Spirit into organic union with Christ its head.

> For just as the body is one and has many members, and all the members of the body, though many, are one body, so it is with Christ. For by one Spirit we were all baptized into one body—Jews or Greeks, slaves or free—and all were made to drink of one Spirit (1 Cor. 12:12-13).

In developing this metaphor, Paul says that the Spirit animates or enlivens the body. The Spirit is a kind of life force. This life force manifests itself in various ways so that, even though there are many diverse members in the body, there is unity—unity in diversity. From Paul we can conclude that "where the Spirit ceases to create and foster community, it is no longer the Spirit of God."[21]

Thus when Paul speaks of the Spirit and the Christian life he most often speaks in communal terms. The Spirit empowers a new kind of love and makes possible a new kind of life for others. The Spirit's gifts are for the purpose of serving "the common good" and building up the body. The fullness of the Spirit thus means, not private spiritual ecstasy, not private enrichment, but the communal confession of Jesus as Lord. It means unreserved submission to his authority and a readiness to live cruciform lives. As Eduard Schweizer put it, "the Holy Spirit makes us receptive to Jesus."[22]

By dwelling in Christ's body, which is the church, the Spirit continues Christ's incarnation. Through the Spirit, Christ remains present. Through the Spirit, Christ comes alive in us. In the power of the Spirit, the church thus ministers to the world in the same ways that Jesus would if he remained physically upon the earth.

Continuing Christ's ministry means, in essence, following the way of the cross. Following that way, as we have seen, requires certain character traits and moral skills. The Spirit, working through the Word and in the community of faith, forms those new traits within us. The Spirit, as we submit to its leading, directs our training in those new skills.

Chief among them is love (1 Cor. 13). Thus Paul can write that "God's love has been poured into our hearts through the Holy Spirit which has been given to us" (Rom. 5:5). In addition the Spirit bears in us the fruit of "joy, peace, patience, kindness, goodness, faithfulness, gentleness, and self-control" (Gal. 5:22-23). It is not that we simply need an extra boost in attaining such traits. For in Paul's view, as Leander Keck notes, the "Spirit is not an aid to doing good. It is rather a realm of power from the new age which creates love if one allows it to."[23] As Paul himself puts it, "If the Spirit is the source of our life, let the Spirit also direct our course" (Gal. 5:26, NEB).

The Spirit-formed, Spirit-led community stands in sharp contrast to worldly communities. Spirit-formed virtues often differ sharply from worldly virtues. As Robert Roberts wrote:

> Love of neighbor is very different from being a jolly good fellow. The peace which passes understanding is almost incomparable with the peace of having one's house mortage paid off. Knowing one's sins to be for-

given is utterly unlike the easy forgetfulness of our guilt encouraged by popular psychology. Trusting in God has hardly anything in common with calculating the probabilities of a successful future.[24]

The Spirit is the life-giving power at work in the body of Christ. Through the Spirit we become a cruciform people, God's new social order. In the power of the Holy Spirit the church stands against the spirit of the age.

Alien Citizens

The church's stance toward the world, as we have seen, involves a great paradox. Early Christians expressed this paradox by speaking of themselves as "alien citizens." It is an image that has deep roots in the New Testament. God's great people of faith "acknowledged that they were strangers and exiles on the earth" (Heb. 11:13). Though Christians are "aliens and exiles," they must "be subject for the Lord's sake to every human institution" (1 Pet. 2:11-14). Though "our commonwealth is in heaven," we live and patiently serve in this world (Phil. 3:20).

In the second-century, pagans puzzled over such attitudes toward the world. They wondered how the Christian church enabled its members "to set little store by this world, and even to make light of death itself." In response, an early Christian writer spoke of this stance as a marvelous paradox:

> ... though they are residents at home in their own countries, their behaviour there is more like that of transients; they take their full part as citizens, but they also submit to anything and everything as if they were aliens. For them, any foreign country is a homeland, and any homeland a foreign country.[25]

Though frequently speaking of themselves as "alien citizens," however, Christians of the first few centuries easily dissolved the paradox. Today, we face the same temptation.

We face temptations in two directions: on the one hand, we are tempted to spiritualize the church and its mission; on the other hand, we are tempted to secularize it. Against an overly spiritualized faith we are called to active, compassionate, sacrificial involvement in the world. And against the secular faith so rampant among us today, we are called to offer not simply a helping hand or various forms of therapy but redemption—a proclamation of the radical human estrangement from God and the transforming power of God's atonement through Christ.

Christians who emphasize separation from the world face a special temptation. As Niebuhr pointed out, they are particularly prone to divide "the world into the material realm governed by a principle opposed to Christ and a spiritual realm guided by the spiritual God."[26]

Such a division brings one perilously close to the ancient gnostic heresy. Christian gnostics of the early Christian era held a dualistic view of the cosmos. They opened up a great chasm between a sordid material world and a glorious spiritual realm. These two realms stood in sharp conflict. The human spirit thus longed for escape from the world of matter into the world of spirit. W. B. Yeats, in his famous poem "Sailing to Byzantium," well described such a view when he spoke of the human spirit as "sick with desire/ and fastened to a dying animal."

Throughout its history the Christian church often has tended toward such a view. It crops up, for example, in Protestant sectarian movements from the sixteenth century all the way down to contemporary American fundamentalism. Wherever such a view appears, it tends to create a community that barricades itself against the assaults of the world. It produces a "wait it out" attitude toward the world—one that says, "Protect yourself, build your walls, mark time until at last you escape into the realms of spiritual bliss."

Such a view always lacks a full biblical doctrine of creation. As Reinhold Niebuhr well put it:

> Every distinction between an essentially good eternity and an essentially evil finiteness is foreign to the Christian faith. When Christians express their faith in such terms, they have been corrupted by other types of religion. For the Christian who really understands his faith, life is really worth living and this world is not merely a "vale of tears." He is able to discern the goodness of creation beneath the corruption of human sin.[27]

Thus when we live as "alien citizens" we do not simply mark time in the world. We do not despise its good gifts or isolate ourselves from its suffering. Far from it. For the cross always points us into the world. The way of the cross always leads us down from life's balcony into its vast arena. But we enter that arena possessing a resurrection hope and thus an "alien" status.

Because of that "alien" status we gain the ability to "sit loose in the world." We live with the firm knowledge that neither this world's apparent threats (persecution, suffering of all kinds, death) nor its many delights are ultimately final. We live with the knowledge that the "powers" of this present age, though they rage around us, sink their teeth and nails into us, and threaten to undo us, are doomed. Finished.

As a result, we can now face them with a certain nonchalance, a kind of lightness. We take the realities of suffering, sin, and death very seriously, but we do not elevate them (as the world does) to the level of ultimate power. We know that death remains the last enemy, so we can never approach suffering people with a glib and condescending cheerfulness. But because we know the truth about these "powers"—that Christ disarmed them, that they no longer rule—we can better face them. We can call their bluff and expose their pretensions. We can boldly announce Christ's lordship over them. And with patience, compassion, and a kind of holy recklessness, we can tend to their victims.

Conclusion

In this chapter I have looked into our past and glimpsed some of our forebearers' struggles with the world—and with a worldly church. I have explored the paradox of standing *against* the world *for* the world and of living as "alien citizens." Through it all, I have insisted that the church—God's new social order—can serve the world most faithfully and sacrificially by being the church.

Now finally I ask what all of this might mean for local congregations—the ones we will meet with next Sunday? How might we address the problem of Christ and culture there? In the barest outline, I offer four suggestions.

(1) *Create channels for closer fellowship and greater involvement with one another.* This will mean greater efforts to get beyond the impersonality of large assemblies and involve people in small groups. It will mean seeking centers of close and intense fellowship—groups on the order of the early Christian "house churches."[28]

(2) *Restore meaningful standards of church membership.* If the church is to be a training ground where people learn to follow the way of the cross, then certain disciplines must be upheld. The church must maintain an environment (or ethos) where Christians can gain the appropriate virtues and learn the necessary moral skills. It must find firm and loving ways to address lifestyles that do not befit God's new social order.

(3) *Make confession of sin a more integral part of the church's life together.* Our gatherings—whether all together for worship or scattered in small groups—need channels of repentance and confession. We need regular times in our public worship to confess, together as a body, that we have sinned, that we have traveled our own way rather than God's. For the church, unlike the world, consists of people who are learning to face up to their sinfulness rather than hide, excuse, or rationalize it. They are learning to confess their selfishness and so open their lives to God and others.

(4) *Sound a call to greater modesty and simplicity of life—and seek leaders who model such a life.* As "strangers and exiles" in this world, Christians are called to travel light. Though we participate in God's great feast of good things, it remains for now a "movable feast." Caravaning, as Vernard Eller put it, remains the appropriate style of the church. So we need leaders experienced in the demands of spiritual travel, leaders who can help us trim down and shape up for the rigors of the road.

Some may say that the way of the cross is too arduous a calling, too demanding an ethic. Some may say it is unreasonable and unworkable. Some may protest that the church simply cannot live such a life in this world. Hearing Jesus' hard demands, some may well ask, with Jesus' first disciples, "Who then can be saved?" Faced with such concerns, beset with such misgivings, we must hear Jesus' answer: "With men this is impossible, but with God all things are possible" (Mt. 19:25).

Only in the power of the Spirit do we find the resources
for following such a way.

O Thou, far off and here, whole and broken,
Who in necessity and in bounty wait,
Whose truth is light and dark, mute though spoken,
By thy wide grace show me thy narrow gate.[29]

Notes

Epigraphs: Augustine, *Exposition on the Book of Psalms* (Oxford, Eng., 1847-57), comment on Psalm 137; Ernst Käsemann, "The Pauline Theology of the Cross," *Interpretation* 24 (April 1970):171.

[1]Ernst Troeltsch, *The Social Teachings of the Christian Churches and Groups,* trans. Olive Wyon (London, Eng.: Allen & Unwin, 1931), 2:993. H. Richard Niebuhr adapted this typology to the American milieu in his book, *The Social Sources of Denominationalism* (New York: Henry Holt, 1929). For an overview of this typology and its development, see David O. Moberg, *The Church as a Social Institution,* 2nd ed. (Grand Rapids, Mich.: Baker, 1984), pp. 73-92.

[2]Donald F. Durnbaugh, *The Believers' Church: The History and Character of Radical Protestantism,* 2nd ed. (Scottdale, Pa.: Herald, 1985), p. 4.

[3]Franklin H. Littell, "The Anabaptist Concept of the Church," in *Recovery of the Anabaptist Vision,* ed. Guy S. Hershberger (Scottdale, Pa.: Herald, 1957), p. 127.

[4]George H. Williams, "'Congregationalist' Luther and the Free Churches," *Lutheran Quarterly* 19 (1967):292.

[5]Richard T. Hughes, "'Christians' in the Early South: The Perspective of Joseph Thomas, 'The White Pilgrim,'" *Discipliana* 46 (Fall 1986):37.

[6]Alexander Campbell, preface, *Millennial Harbinger,* new series, 7 (1843):6-7; C. L. Loos, "A Chapter in Art-History in Churches," ibid. 39 (1868):282.

[7]Alexander Campbell, "Morality of Christians—No. XX," *Millennial Harbinger,* New Series, 4 (June 1840):275.

[8]David E. Harrell, *Quest for a Christian America* (Nashville, Tenn.: Disciples of Christ Historical Society, 1966), p. 293.

⁹David Lipscomb, "A Visit to Chattanooga," *Gospel Advocate* (April 3, 1889):214.

¹⁰John Allen Hudson, "My Work with the Union Avenue Church," *Gospel Advocate* 67 (December 3, 1925):1158.

¹¹James A. Allen, response to Hudson, ibid., pp. 1158-59. I am indebted to Don Haymes for his analysis of this episode [in "The Road More Traveled: How the Churches of Christ became a Denomination," *Mission Journal* (March 1987):4-8].

¹²H. Richard Niebuhr, *Christ and Culture* (New York: Harper & Row, 1951). The quotes in the following six paragraphs come from pp. 41, 42, 155, 156, and 215.

¹³John Howard Yoder, "The Otherness of the Church," *Mennonite Quarterly Review* 35 (October 1961):286-96, and *The Priestly Kingdom: Social Ethics as Gospel* (Notre Dame, Ind.: University of Notre Dame, 1984), pp. 135-47. On the continued influence of the Constantinian model of church/world relations, see Stanley Hauerwas, "A Christian Critique of Christian America," in *Christian Existence Today: Essays on Church, World, and Living in Between* (Durham, N.C.: Labyrinth, 1988), pp. 180-84.

¹⁴Yoder argues that Niebuhr's "fundamental Christ/culture polarity and typology of possible ethical standards which he builds upon it, are at bottom unfair to history and unfruitful for ethics. The reason for this is the assumption that culture 'as such,' i.e., as distinct from Christ, is a tangible reality capable of being related consistently to Christ in one of the five typical ways. This is to attribute to the world that intrinsic ontological dignity which neither the New Testament nor history allows it to claim" ["Otherness of the Church," p. 294].

¹⁵Herman Sasse, "*Kosmos*," in *Theological Dictionary of the New Testament*, ed. Gerhard Kittel, trans. Geoffrey W. Bromiley (Grand Rapids, Mich.: Eerdmans, 1965), 3:893; C. H. Dodd, *The Johannine Epistles* (New York: Harpers, 1946), p. xxxi.

¹⁶Robin Scroggs, *Paul for a New Day* (Philadelphia, Pa.: Fortress, 1977), p. 52.

¹⁷Stanley Hauerwas, *The Peaceable Kingdom: A Primer in Christian Ethics* (Notre Dame, Ind.: University of Notre Dame, 1983), pp. 101-102.

¹⁸Peter Riedeman, *Account of Our Religion, Doctrine and Faith*, quoted in *Anabaptism in Outline: Selected Primary Sources*, ed. Walter Klassen (Scottdale, Pa.: Herald, 1981), p. 112.

[19]Frederick H. Kanfer, "Personal Control, Social Control, and Altruism: Can Society Survive the Age of Individualism," *American Psychologist* 34 (March 1979):237. Kanfer notes that "current clinical practices tend to emphasize therapeutic objectives of personal self-fulfillment, self-sufficiency, and independence from social systems" (p. 237).

[20]On the controversies over the Spirit's indwelling in the individual, see Patrick Brooks, "Lockean Epistemology and the Indwelling Spirit in the Restoration Movement" (M.A. thesis, Abilene Christian University, 1977).

[21]Eduard Schweizer, *The Holy Spirit*, trans. Reginald and Ilse Fuller (Philadelphia, Pa.: Fortress, 1980), p. 91. On Paul's use of the "body" metaphor, see Ralph P. Martin, *The Spirit and the Congregation: Studies in 1 Corinthians 12-15* (Grand Rapids, Mich.: Eerdmans, 1984), pp. 21-34.

[22]Schweizer, *The Holy Spirit*, p. 126.

[23]Leander E. Keck, "Justification of the Ungodly and Ethics," in *Rechtfertigung*, ed. Johannes Friedrich, et. al. (Tübingen: Mohr, 1976), p. 202.

[24]Robert C. Roberts, "Faith and Modern Humanity: Two Approaches," *Christian Century* (March 29, 1978): 331.

[25]*Epistle of Diognetus* 5. 5 [English translation by Rowan A. Greer]. On the use of this theme in the early Christian era, see Greer, *Broken Lights and Mended Lives: Theology and Common Life in the Early Church* (University Park, Pa.: Pennsylvania State University, 1986), pp. 141-61.

[26]H. Richard Niebuhr, *Christ and Culture*, p. 81.

[27]Reinhold Niebuhr, *Beyond Tragedy: Essays on the Christian Interpretation of History* (New York: Charles Scribner's Sons, 1937), p. 132.

[28]See Del Birkey, *The House Church: A Model for Renewing the Church* (Scottdale, Pa.: Herald, 1989).

[29]Wendell Berry, "To the Holy Spirit," in *Collected Poems* (San Francisco, Calif.: North Point, 1985), p. 209.

The Ordeal of Compassion

. . . there is nothing heavier than compassion. Not even one's own pain feels so heavy as the pain one feels with someone, for someone, a pain intensified by the imagination and prolonged by a hundred echoes.
—*Milan Kundera (1984)*

The heart is stretched through suffering, and enlarged. But O the agony of this enlarging of the heart, that one may be prepared to enter into the anguish of others!
—*Thomas Kelly (1941)*

Cruciform Virtues

A fundamental mark of the church's identity is the quality and character of the lives of its members. Jesus said to his disciples: "A new commandment I give to you, that you love one another; even as I have loved you, that you also love one another. By this all men will know that you are my disciples, if you have love for one another" (Jn. 13:34-35; cf. 1 Jn. 3:16-18).

Because Christians have "become partakers of the divine nature," their lives are distinguished by faith, virtue, knowledge, self-control, steadfastness, godliness, brotherly affection, and love (2 Pet. 1:5-7). Beginning at baptism, they put on the garments of compassion, lowliness, meekness, forbearance, forgiveness, and love. As members of the one body, Christ's peace rules their lives (Col 3:12-15).

The church of Jesus Christ will be identified most clearly by the character of its people. The church is not primarily an association of people who know and defend the basic teachings of the Christian faith, people who pride themselves on knowing precisely what one must believe. Rather, the church is God's new creation, a people who have Christ formed in them, who walk by the Spirit and crucify the flesh.

The Scriptures do not separate doctrine from ethics. As Jaroslav Pelikan put it, "when the Old Testament speaks about 'instruction' or the New Testament about 'doctrine,' this includes both confession and conduct, both theology and ethics." He adds that a "separation between them is fatal."[1] We might say that in Scripture ethics and doctrine are so woven together that one cannot even find a seam between them.

But fairly early in Christian history they began to be wedged apart. Church leaders began to distinguish "the precision of dogmas" from "the ethical part." Though both were viewed as important, doctrine and ethics nonetheless drifted apart. As a measure of orthodoxy, doctrinal precision took its place well above ethics; the profession of truth superseded the practice of truth. Throughout the succeeding centuries Christians have tended to separate belief and practice, doctrine and life, words and the realities to which words point.

Throughout their history, Churches of Christ have tended to uphold such a distinction. Though never denying the importance of the righteous life, Churches of Christ have usually made precision of doctrine far more the test of orthodoxy than Christlikeness. When Moses Lard, for example, stated that one departure from the New Testament pattern made one "an apostate from our ranks" (as we saw in chapter two), he was not talking so much about how people lived but about what they believed and what they practiced in church. He was talking about precision of doctrine, not about quality of life.

This separation between doctrine and life has created a narrow and stunted measure of orthodoxy. A church can be "sound" while excluding black people from its midst. A church can be doctrinally correct while virtually ignoring the poor and hungry living down the street. Christians may pride themselves on their soundness in the faith while hoarding their money or vilifying their brother or brutalizing their family or splitting churches. People may argue endlessly about the proper way to care for orphans while largely failing to care for orphans.

Orthodoxy involves confession and conduct. It involves right living just as much as it involves right thinking. Sound doctrine entails caring for the neighbor just as much as knowing the place of baptism. It entails welcoming people of all races and stations into our fellowship as much as affirming that "God is no respector of persons." It calls for compassion as much as for confession.

Christlike character is the indelible mark of the true body of Christ. As Stanley Hauerwas concluded, "The church is finally known by the character of the people who constitute it, and if we lack that character, the world rightly draws the conclusion that the God we worship is in fact a false God."[2]

The church that lives under the cross will consist of people possessing cruciform virtues, that is, the character traits and virtues necessary to follow the way of the cross. The way of the cross is an arduous, demanding way. It calls for people with certain strengths, specific traits. It calls for patience and endurance, courage and fortitude. It especially calls for people with hope—as Paul says, suffering produces endurance, endurance produces character, and character hope (Rom. 5:3-5).

As we saw in the previous chapter, we gain these virtues in God's new social order, the church. For there a different, Spirit-empowered ethos prevails. There, in the power of the Spirit, we place ourselves under God's discipline and experience his training in righteousness. There we acquire the cruciform virtues.

Prominent among these cruciform virtues is compassion—the ability to enter into the experiences of another, particularly the sufferings of another. Of all the virtues we might seek, this one brings us closest to the mind of Christ. As we become compassionate people our hearts begin to beat with the heart of God. For this reason, I focus in this chapter on the virtue of compassion.

The Heaviest Virtue

(1) *Compassion begins with understanding.* To feel with another, to share another's suffering, one must first know something of the burden pressing upon the person. But such knowledge must not be confused with simple analytical knowledge, with a body of facts, for that is incomplete and too easily taken lightly or dismissed. I refer, rather, to a kind of personal knowing where one sees oneself in the other, where ones knows the sting of despair, the heaviness of grief, or the lightness of joy.

True understanding will mean listening longer and, in the process, setting aside (at least for a while) some of our ready-made answers to the riddles of life. It will mean hearing out the questions without immediately defusing them with the answers. It will mean, in short, exposing oneself to the anxiety of unresolved dilemmas. We miss, for example, Abraham's terror in heeding God's call to sacrifice Isaac because we read the story already knowing about the ram in the thicket. We are impatient to apply the end to the beginning; as a result we miss the intensity of the struggle through knowledge of the victory.

It is this very temptation that haunts us. We are tempted to live too easily, too smugly with the gospel. We find ourselves drawn, like the early Corinthians, to a theology of glory that eclipses the theology of the cross. We find ourselves climbing out of the arena and taking refuge in the balcony. There we grow content with Band-Aid-like remedies, with rapid-fire answers scattered about like machine gun bullets on the arena below.

God's reconciling people cannot forget that deep understanding precedes healing love and compassion. "Tell me how much you know of the sufferings of your fellowman," Helmut Thielecke wrote, "and I will tell you how much you love them."[3]

(2) *Understanding must deepen into a willingness to bear the burden that such understanding brings.* The exercise of compassion means not turning away from another's pain or grief or failure because one finds it unsettling or even sickening. It means refusing oneself the indulgence of sentimentality. "To sentimentalize something," Frederick Buechner wrote, "is to look only at the emotion in it and at the emotion it stirs in us rather than at the reality of it."[4] Being compassionate means

looking past the feelings—which we so easily turn to selfish ends anyway—and focusing clearly and steadfastly on the situation itself.

Two Greek words in the New Testament indicate that compassion involves a sense of anger or outrage. One word, weakly translated "compassion" and used in classical Greek to describe the seat of a person's deepest emotions, denotes anger at the situation that has reduced a person to his present circumstances. A second word is used twice in the Fourth Gospel to describe Jesus' reaction at Lazarus' tomb ("deeply moved," Jn. 11:33, 38). Jesus was both deeply stirred and angered by the inexorable power of death.

The ordeal of compassionate ministry lies precisely in the fact that it engages one's whole being, even to the point of anxiety and outrage.

(3) *Compassion finally involves identification with the sufferings of another.* For God it led first to the incarnation (or "enfleshment"), then to the cross. We might say that Jesus in the flesh was the highest expression of the divine compassion. For his disciples the way of compassion means the way of cross-bearing, a willingness to enter into the experience of others. It means a readiness to bear with the weakness and pain of another because one knows such weakness and pain as potentially one's own.

In this seeing of oneself in the other we come to the heart of compassion. Robert Roberts says it well:

> When I perceive someone compassionately, the weakness or suffering or sin I see in him is a quality I see also in myself. . . . In this understanding, the sins of others cease to be inscrutable abysses of alien darkness and look instead like mirrors in which we see our deepest selves. . . . I too am susceptible to the suffering I see in this other, I too am weak and deficient in many ways, I too will soon die, I too am a sinner in need of forgiveness—when these considerations issue in helpfulness, patience, mercy, and gentleness, then compassion has prevailed.[5]

How is such identification with others possible? How is it possible to get outside of ourselves enough to know and feel what others experience? How can we see the weakness and failure of others as potentially our own?

In his famous novel *The Power and the Glory*, Graham Greene gives us a clue. The story takes place in Mexico at a time when priests and other religious leaders were being purged. Most of them have fled the country or have been captured.

The story focuses on one priest who has remained behind out of a sense of loyalty to his flock. The authorities finally capture him and throw him into a dark, crowded, stinking jail. During the night a raucus old woman (who has discovered his identity) accuses him of being a bad priest because, she says, "you sympathize with these animals." "The sooner you are dead," she concludes, "the better."

Greene then describes the priest's reaction:

> He couldn't see her in the darkness, but there were plenty of faces he could remember from the old days which fitted the voice. When you visualized a man or woman carefully you could always begin to feel pity. . . That was a quality God's image carried with it. . . . When you saw the lines at the corners of the eyes, the shape of the mouth, how the hair grew, it was impossible to hate. Hate was just a failure of the imagination. He began again to feel an enormous responsibility for this pious woman.[6]

Here we have a basic clue to the virtue of compassion—imagination. Mistreatment of another human being results, in part, from a failure of imagination. It results from failing to see or imagine oneself in the other person.

Compassion, according to Lawrence Blum, involves an "imaginative dwelling on the condition of the other person." This imaginative identification does not necessarily require that one have experienced the same things. That can certainly promote compassion. Someone who has lost a child can readily feel the pain of someone else who has lost a child. Compassion is natural in such a situation.

But compassion is not limited to those who share similar experiences. It does not require that we be able to say, "I understand what you are going through because I have suffered the same thing myself." Rather, it calls for imagination. It involves "imagining what the other person, given his character, beliefs, and values, is undergoing, rather than what we ourselves would feel in his situation."

The point is that imagination is a necessary condition for compassion. It involves an imaginative leap beyond oneself into the life of another, one who may well be very different from oneself. Thus Blum notes that "expanding our powers of imagination expands our capacity for compassion. And conversely the limits of a person's capacities for imaginative reconstruction set limits on her capacity for compassion."[7]

Precisely here is where the loss of metaphor and image in our reading of Scripture has had such dire spiritual consequences. As we saw in chapters two and three, our traditional way of reading the Bible sought to boil down metaphorical language to factual language, to excise verbal images and figures of speech. As James Lamar put it, one must eliminate the Bible's "highly-colored imagery and bold hyperboles." The "poetic element" must be "rendered simple." For the true biblical doctrine resides only in the "facts."

But it is through metaphor, image, and figure of speech that we exercise our imaginations—and thus develop the capacity to enter imaginatively into the experiences of others. Cynthia Ozick, acclaimed novelist and essayist, argues that "metaphor is one of the chief agents of our moral nature, and that the more serious we are in life, the less we can do without it." Metaphor enables us to imagine what it is like to be someone else, to live in another time and place. "Through metaphor, the past has the capacity to imagine us, and we it."[8] Metaphor forges links between the strange and the familiar. Many of the Christian virtues rest on such a capacity.

Ozick tells of the time she was invited to read some of her work before an assembly of physicians. The story she read was a kind of parable. It was a story, she said, "drenched in metaphor." But it was not well received. "They wanted plain speech," Ozick observed. "They were appalled by metaphor, by fable, image, echo, irony, satire, the call to interpret, the call to penetrate. . . ." They were serious, scientific people trained in technique, trafficking in precision, and so were put off by metaphor.

Reflecting on the event, Ozick suggests that metaphor is an intruder in our lives—it "instigates reckless cliff-walking; it sweeps its quarry to the edge of unfamiliar abysses." It takes us places we may not want to go, into lives and experiences we may find burdensome. But precisely for this reason, metaphor also makes compassion possible.

> Through metaphorical concentration, doctors can imagine what it is to be their patients. Those who have no pain can imagine those who suffer. Those at the center can imagine what it is to be outside. The strong can imagine what it is to be weak. Illuminated lives can imagine the dark. Poets in their twilight can imagine the borders of stellar fire. We strangers can imagine the familiar hearts of strangers.[9]

From Pride to Compassion

I turn now to one broad phenomenon that significantly blocks truly compassionate ministry. While we could focus on psychological factors, and explore such things as how early family experiences inhibit the capacity to give and receive love, I propose rather a theological factor: the widespread tendency to reduce the Christian life and message to an oversimplified, over-rationalized system devoid of paradox and mystery.

This reductionism takes many forms. In its basic form it springs from a longing for simplicity. The gospel becomes a piece of information, an outline, a five-point plan. In this view every complex problem has a simple answer. Find a text, memorize a few Bible verses, go to a workshop, get the latest religious bestseller. All the answers are there. You can discover the fullness of salvation on your coffee break. You can find the key to life while waiting for the light to change. Never mind, as Donald Baillie observed, that "most of the great [Christian] heresies arose from an undue desire for simplification, an undue impatience with mystery and paradox, and an endeavour after a common-sense theology."[10]

We readily abolish mystery due to what William Barrett has called a "totalitarianism of the mind."

We become totalitarians of the mind; but we ourselves are our own victims, for we have imprisoned ourselves in a total ideology beyond which we cannot see. We are no longer free to let things be what they are, but must twist them to fit into the framework we impose. . . . Why? Because, like children afraid of the dark, we cannot abide to stand within mystery, and so must have a truth that is total.[11]

Thus we are tempted to reduce the "heights and depths" of our faith to the knee-deep shallows, the "unsearchable riches" to a bargain basement sale, the high mystery to a simple set of propositions.

A basic problem with such reductionism lies in the attitude it generates toward others. If indeed everything is so simple, then those who differ with us must be either extremely dense or hopelessly obstinate. Such an attitude results in an authoritarianism and dogmatism leading to the end of thought rather than to the birth of thought, to a call for subjugation rather than free and ongoing investigation.

Behind such authoritarianism lies an inability to comes to terms with one's own humanness. We easily fall prey to the illusion that by condemning human weakness and ignorance long enough or loudly enough we can lift ourselves above it. Unable to admit our own weaknesses and doubts, we find it hard to muster compassionate concern for those who doubt. Unable to face our own vulnerability to evil, we lift ourselves above those who struggle in its grasp.

Being truly compassionate means acknowledging our own full creatureliness. It means, as Augustine put it, getting to the point where one can say, "I count nothing human foreign to myself." In doing that we will relieve the tensions that result from pretensions about ourselves. "Be not angry," wrote Thomas `a Kempis, "that you cannot make others as you wish them to be, since you cannot make yourself as you wish to be."[12]

The Christian story is the story of Emmanuel—God with us. That story tells of a God who did not just come near us but of a God who became one of us. God chose through Christ to take on human creatureliness with all its susceptibility to pain and death. God chose to take on the whole range of human griefs and joys. And God even chose to take on, in some mysterious sense, our sin. Paul wrote, "For our sake he made him to be sin who knew no sin, so that in him we might become the righteousness of God" (2 Cor. 5:21).

In Jesus, God chose to extend himself. God chose to broaden himself to take part in our condition. God, we might say, is broad-minded. God's broadmindedness does not mean an easy acceptance of sin. It does not mean a careless attitude toward human behavior. It means rather that, though God abhors sin, he refuses to remain separated from us even for that reason. In fact, God came near us and identified with us precisely because of our weakness, suffering, and sin.

This compassionate incarnation of God in Christ stands at the center of the Christian faith. It is not simply one doctrine among others. It is not simply a gospel "fact" to be believed. Rather, it provides the dominant model for all Christian behavior. It is the grand vision by which we live. It is the inexhaustible mystery that captivates and compels us, a scene so beautiful, true, and good that it draws our gaze away from our own small lives and halting moral efforts. It draws us out of ourselves. With our gaze fixed steadily there, we find ourselves drawn more and more into a breadth of mercy and compassion that reflects, however dimly, the compassion of God.

Accepting God's mercy through Jesus Christ means committing oneself to striving for broadness in our mercy to others. Such broadness must not be confused with the weakness of character that cares little for truth and goodness. It is not the kind of broadness that characterizes the weakhearted and morally confused. Rather, this broadness requires great strength of character. It requires spirit-formed virtues. For accepting God's mercy means going further than we had ever considered going in identifying ourselves with weak, suffering, or sinful people.

"For this reason," as Robert Roberts insists, "the Christian community does not settle for whatever compassion comes naturally, but educates for it. It holds constantly before itself the tender stooping love of God and by so doing constantly seeks to stretch the self-concepts of its individual members into a broadmindedness imitative of its Lord's."[13]

This means that we must be prepared, as Thomas Merton pointed out, to make our way into a desert, desolate and hopeless, and there cultivate a garden. "What is my new desert?" Merton asked. "The name of it is compassion. There is no wilderness so terrible, so beautiful, so arid and so fruitful as the wilderness of compassion. . . . It is in the desert of compassion that the thirsty land turns into springs of water, that the poor possess all things."[14]

Here lies the central paradox: healing begins in identification with the pain; it begins in the desert. With the vision of Christ ever before us, we take our stance beside, not above, those who sin and who suffer. We become ever more acutely aware that we harbor in our own lives the same possibilities for evil and pain and that only by a remarkable grace are we new creations.

Only as this awareness deepens does pride give way to compassion. And only as pride gives way to compassion will we become a cruciform church.

Notes

Epigraphs: Milan Kundera, *The Unbearable Lightness of Being* (New York: Harper & Row, 1984), p. 31; Thomas Kelly, *A Testament of Devotion* (New York: Harper & Brothers, 1941), p. 71.

[1]Jaroslav Pelikan, *The Christian Tradition: A History of the Development of Doctrine* (Chicago, Ill.: University of Chicago, 1971), 1:2-3.

[2]Stanley Hauerwas, *The Peaceable Kingdom* (Notre Dame, Ind.: University of Notre Dame, 1983), p. 109.

[3]Helmut Thielecke, *Our Heavenly Father* (New York: Harper & Row, 1960), p. 93.

[4]Frederick Buechner, *Telling the Truth* (New York: Harper & Row, 1977), p. 36.

[5]Robert C. Roberts, *Spirituality and Human Emotion* (Grand Rapids, Mich.: Eerdmans, 1982), pp. 110-11, 40.

⁶Graham Greene, *The Power and the Glory* (New York: Bantam, 1972), p. 123.

⁷Lawrence Blum, "Compassion," in *Explaining Emotions*, ed. Amelie O. Rorty (Berkeley, Calif.: University of California, 1980), pp. 510-11.

⁸Cynthia Ozick, *Metaphor and Memory* (New York: Alfred Knopf, 1989), pp. 265-69.

⁹Ibid., p. 283.

¹⁰Donald Baillie, *God Was in Christ* (New York: Scribner's, 1948), p. 65.

¹¹William Barrett, *The Illusion of Technique: A Search for Meaning in a Technological Society* (Garden City, N.Y.: Doubleday, 1978), pp. 149-50.

¹²Thomas `a Kempis, *The Imitation of Christ* 1. 16.

¹³Roberts, *Spirituality*, p. 120. In the four preceding paragraphs I am indebted to Roberts discussion.

¹⁴Thomas Merton, *The Sign of Jonas* (Garden City, N.Y.: Doubleday, 1956), p. 323.

Index